BIOSPHERE

Ecosystems and Biodiversity Loss

OUR FRAGILE PLANET

BIOSPHERE

Ecosystems and Biodiversity Loss

DANA DESONIE, PH.D.

CHELSEA HOUSE
PUBLISHERS
An imprint of Infobase Publishing

Chelsea House
An imprint of Infobase Publishing
132 West 31st Street
New York NY 10001

Library of Congress Cataloging-in-Publication Data
Desonie, Dana.
   Biosphere : ecosystems and biodiversity loss / Dana Desonie.
      p. cm.—(Our fragile planet)
   Includes bibliographical references and index.
   ISBN-13: 978–0-8160–6219–5 (hardcover)
   ISBN-10: 0–8160–6219–6 (hardcover)
  1. Biosphere—Juvenile literature.   2. Biotic communities—Juvenile literature.   3. Biodiversity conservation—Juvenile literature.   I. Title. II. Series.
   QH343.4.D47 2007
   333.95—dc22   2007016921

Chelsea House books are available at special discounts when purchased in bulk quantities for businesses, associations, institutions, or sales promotions. Please call our Special Sales Department in New York at (212) 967–8800 or (800) 322–8755.

You can find Chelsea House on the World Wide Web at http://www.chelseahouse.com

Text design by Annie O'Donnell
Cover design by Ben Peterson

Printed in the United States of America

Bang NMSG 10 9 8 7 6 5 4 3 2 1

This book is printed on acid-free paper.

All links and Web addresses were checked and verified to be correct at the time of publication. Because of the dynamic nature of the Web, some addresses and links may have changed since publication and may no longer be valid.

Cover photograph: © Martin Harvey / Photo Researchers, Inc.

Contents

Preface

The planet is a marvelous place: a place with blue skies, wild storms, deep lakes, and rich and diverse ecosystems. The tides ebb and flow, baby animals are born in the spring, and tropical rain forests harbor an astonishing array of life. The Earth sustains living things and provides humans with the resources to maintain a bountiful way of life: water, soil, and nutrients to grow food, and the mineral and energy resources to build and fuel modern society, among many other things.

The physical and biological sciences provide an understanding of the whys and hows of natural phenomena and processes—why the sky is blue and how metals form, for example—and insights into how the many parts are interrelated. Climate is a good example. Among the many influences on the Earth's climate are the circulation patterns of the atmosphere and the oceans, the abundance of plant life, the quantity of various gases in the atmosphere, and even the sizes and shapes of the continents. Clearly, to understand climate it is necessary to have a basic understanding of several scientific fields and to be aware of how these fields are interconnected.

As Earth scientists like to say, the only thing constant about our planet is change. From the ball of dust, gas, and rocks that came together 4.6 billion years ago to the lively and diverse globe that orbits the Sun today, very little about the Earth has remained the same for long. Yet, while change is fundamental, people have altered the environment unlike any other species in Earth's history. Everywhere there are reminders of our presence. A look at the sky might show a sooty cloud or a jet contrail. A look at the sea might reveal plastic refuse, oil, or only a few fish swimming where once they had been countless. The land has been deforested and strip-mined. Rivers and lakes have been polluted. Changing conditions and habitats have caused some plants and animals to expand their populations, while others have become extinct. Even the climate—which for millennia was thought to be beyond human influence—has been shifting due to alterations in the makeup of atmospheric gases brought about by human activities. The planet is changing fast and people are the primary cause.

OUR FRAGILE PLANET is a set of eight books that celebrate the wonders of the world by highlighting the scientific processes behind them. The books also look at the science underlying the tremendous influence humans are having on the environment. The set is divided into volumes based on the large domains on which humans have had an impact: *Atmosphere, Climate, Hydrosphere, Oceans, Geosphere, Biosphere,* and *Polar Regions.* The volume *Humans and the Natural Environment* describes the impact of human activity on the planet and explores ways in which we can live more sustainably.

A core belief expressed in each volume is that to mitigate the impacts humans are having on the Earth, each of us must understand the scientific processes that operate in the natural world. We must understand how human activities disrupt those processes and use that knowledge to predict ways that changes in one system will affect seemingly unrelated systems. These books express the belief that science is the solid ground from which we can reach an agreement on the behavioral changes that we must adopt—both as individuals and as a society—to solve the problems caused by the impact of humans on our fragile planet.

Acknowledgments

I would like to thank, above all, the scientists who have dedicated their lives to the study of the Earth, especially those engaged in the important work of understanding how human activities are impacting the planet. Many thanks to the staff of Facts On File and Chelsea House for their guidance and editing expertise: Frank Darmstadt, Executive Editor; Brian Belval, Senior Editor; and Leigh Ann Cobb, independent developmental editor. Dr. Tobi Zausner located the color images that illustrate our planet's incredible beauty and the harsh reality of the effects human activities are having on it. Thanks also to my agent, Jodie Rhodes, who got me involved in this project.

Family and friends were a great source of support and encouragement as I wrote these books. Special thanks to the May '97 Moms, who provided the virtual water cooler that kept me sane during long days of writing. Cathy Propper was always enthusiastic as I was writing the books, and even more so when they were completed. My mother, Irene Desonie, took great care of me as I wrote for much of June 2006. Mostly importantly, my husband, Miles Orchinik, kept things moving at home when I needed extra writing time and provided love, support, and encouragement when I needed that, too. This book is dedicated to our children, Reed and Maya, who were always loving, and usually patient. I hope these books do a small bit to help people understand how their actions impact the future for all children.

Introduction

Scientists are searching for signs of life elsewhere in the solar system and in the Milky Way galaxy. Rovers, probes, orbiters, and flybys analyze the surface of Mars for the remains of microbes that may once have inhabited a wetter, more hospitable planet. Probes scan for evidence that tiny life forms lie beneath the Red Planet's soil. Spacecraft study Jupiter's moon Europa for confirmation of a salt ocean where life might reside beneath the satellite's thick crust of ice. Spacecraft also look at Jupiter's Ganymede and Saturn's Titan moons for conditions that are—or once might have been—favorable for life. SETI (Search for Extraterrestrial Intelligence) scientists program sensitive receivers to scan the galaxy for radio waves that could only have been produced by intelligent beings.

So far, no extraterrestrial life has been found. At this time, Earth is the only planet known to harbor life; it is the only planet that has a biosphere. Not only is Earth inhabited, it is inhabited on a grand scale, with an unimaginable diversity of life forms. There is hardly a location or set of conditions that does not have an organism that has evolved to live in it. Viruses invade the cells of other organisms. The fungi that cause athlete's foot (*Trichophyton*) thrive in the damp spots between a person's toes. Epiphytes grow atop other plants. Tuna race across the oceans in search of their prey. Giraffes munch leaves no other animals can reach. Desert beetles collect dew on their bodies as their only source of water. Bats snap insects from the air. Humans use intelligence to gather food, avoid predators, and create comfortable living and working environments.

Organisms live together in varied and unique ecosystems. Coral reef ecosystems are supported by the structure created by small coral animals that build their homes on top of one another; such as reef ecosystems are inhabited by an incredible assortment of fish and invertebrates. The scrubby plants of the tundra support a diverse array of birds and large mammals, many of which migrate out of the area for the frigid winters. Desert animals survive long droughts by utilizing the water found in seeds, fruits, or bodies of well-adapted desert plants. The most amazing biodiversity is found in the tropical rain forests, where temperatures are moderate, water is often abundant, and food is plentiful. Every sort of creature—including creeping vines, flying birds, swinging monkeys, and bacteria—all make their homes in and on the varied trees of the rain forest.

The Earth's natural biological systems perform essential services for the planet. Plants convert the Sun's energy to food energy that can be used by other organisms and provide homes in which other organisms can live. Wetlands ecosystems filter water, provide flood control, and serve as nurseries for fish and other animals. Tropical rain forests absorb carbon dioxide and thus keep global temperatures from rising. Humans use the Earth's biodiversity for food, clothing, shelter, medicines, and fuel.

Intentionally or not, human activities alter and sometimes destroy organisms and ecosystems. Most biodiversity is lost as ecosystems are mowed down to make room for human landscapes—homes, farms, power plants, and industrial complexes, for example. Ecosystems may be degraded by being fragmented, as when roads are carved through them, or by being polluted. Hunters and fishers overharvest their prey, sometimes leaving behind only a tiny fraction of the original number of animals. Loggers level forests for the timber and herb collectors deplete the supply of herbaceous plants. Where humans go, other species—rats, cats, fish, and weeds, among many others—follow, whether invited or not. These invaders may devour, outcompete, or run out the ecosystem's native organisms. Climate change also damages ecosystems and species such as when conditions change too rapidly for the organisms to adapt to them. As a result, species extinctions are occurring at a rate 10 to 100 times higher than was normal in the planet's recent history.

Preserving biodiversity should be one of the major concerns of the twenty-first century. Laws are in place to protect species, both nationally and internationally, although sometimes those laws are not enforced. Zoos and other organizations save individual organisms or their genetic material. Lands are preserved as well; some are set aside to remain untouched for all time, while others are integrated into community activities and used sustainably. While efforts are being made to save species and ecosystems, much more must be done if most of the species that are alive today are to be around at the end of the century.

Part One of this book describes the enormous diversity of life on the Earth and the evolutionary processes that created that diversity. The interactions of the organisms between themselves and within their ecosystems are also discussed. The first chapter of Part Two describes the extinctions of organisms throughout the Earth's history; the section's remaining chapters each look at one of the causes of extinctions today. Part Three describes some of the ways people are working to save the planet's diversity of species and ecosystems.

PART ONE

EVOLUTION, ORGANISMS, AND ECOSYSTEMS

The Origin and Evolution of Life

L ife began roughly 4 billion years ago, when the newly formed planet Earth became cool enough to support liquid water, a crust, and an atmosphere. Initially, the simple organisms that came into existence in the watery environment consumed the **organic** (carbon-bearing) **molecules** floating around them. Over enormous amounts of time, simple organisms evolved into more complex organisms. Some developed the ability to turn nutrients and solar energy into food energy. Others could not produce their own food but acquired the ability to use the food energy manufactured by others. These important advances in the history of life allowed the evolution of the enormous diversity of life forms—the **biodiversity**—that make up the Earth's **biosphere** today.

WHAT IS LIFE?

Philosophers, theologians, and others may argue about what **life** is, but biologists recognize life by what it does. To be alive, a material must:

⊕ be able to grow

⊕ be able to transform organic molecules into more complex forms

⊕ organize those molecules into more complex structures, such as **cells** (the smallest unit in a living organism that is capable of engaging in the essential life processes); **tissues** (a group of cells organized to perform a specific function); **organs** (a group of tissues that forms a distinct structure and performs a specialized task, such as a heart in animals or a leaf in plants); and, ultimately, organisms.

⊕ have a **metabolism** (the sum of all the biochemical processes necessary for life) to ensure its individual survival

⊕ reproduce to ensure the long-term survival of the species (**reproduction** is the ability of an organism to create an organism similar to itself. Members of the same **species** can mate and produce fertile offspring).

⊕ have the ability to respond to and adapt to its environment (an **adaptation** is a structure or behavior alteration that can be passed from one generation to the next).

THE ORIGIN OF LIFE

A few ingredients were needed for life to originate on Earth: liquid water, a solid surface (crust) for the water to rest on, a breathable layer of gases (**atmosphere**), and organic molecules. Before complex life could form, protection from the Sun's high-energy **ultraviolet radiation (UV)** was needed, as well. While these commodities are abundant on the Earth now, some of them were scarce when the planet formed 4.6 billion years ago.

Like the other planets in the solar system, Earth formed as chunks of space debris—rocky **asteroids** and balls of rock, ice, and gases called **comets**—were attracted to one another by gravity and smashed together to form into a unified mass. The early planet was too hot to form crust; water and gases were vaporized and lost. Once the planet cooled, perhaps 300 million years after its formation, crust solidified and gases formed an atmosphere. **Water vapor** (the gaseous form of water) made clouds and then precipitated as rain. Basins in the crust collected water. Organic molecules trapped within the ices of comets flew to the planet.

With a crust, atmosphere, and water, the planet was ready for life to originate. The first step would have been generation of complex organic molecules. How this happened is very difficult to discern since little evidence of this process remains. However, through experiments and extensive study on existing organisms, scientists have developed two detailed hypotheses. (A **hypothesis** is a tentative explanation that must be tested further to be verified or disproved.) For decades, the favored hypothesis has been that life began in the early oceans, which contained water, carbon, hydrogen, nitrogen, oxygen, salts, and even **amino acids** (simple organic molecules that are the building blocks of proteins). All that was needed to unite the simple organic molecules into complex ones was a spark of energy, which would have been available from lightning or a nearby volcanic eruption.

In the last few decades, a new hypothesis has been gaining acceptance: that life began at **hydrothermal vents,** hot springs located in volcanic areas on the ocean floor. Nowadays at these sites, scalding water—with temperatures up to 750°F (400°C), laden with minerals and possibly amino acids—shoots from the vents into cold seawater. In the early Earth, complex organic molecules could have synthesized from the simple organic molecules coming from the vents and the vent's heat. The most important line of evidence in support of this hypothesis is that the most primitive organisms on the Earth are the **thermophilic** (heat-loving) bacteria that now thrive in hot vent waters. (**Bacteria** are microscopic, single-celled organisms that live in an incredible diversity of environments.)

Complex organic molecules then surrounded themselves with a membrane, thereby keeping the materials they needed always available and keeping out oxygen, which is poison to simple biochemical reactions. In this way, the first cells formed. Cells may come together to form a complex organism, or a single cell may be an entire creature. Every cell contains a **nucleus,** which directs the cell's important functions. Every nucleus contains **nucleic acids**, organic substances that are important for storing and replicating hereditary information for the next generation. The nucleic acid that carries hereditary information in higher organisms is **deoxyribonucleic acid (DNA)**. DNA makes an identical copy of itself, so that when the cell divides, each daughter cell receives the genetic information from the parent. One of life's crucial developments was the ability to reproduce and pass on its genetic material to its offspring.

The first cells were very simple **prokaryotes**, single-celled organisms, such as bacteria, that lack a membrane-bound nucleus. For food, the earliest organisms just took in small amounts of the organic molecules that were nearby and digested them using fermentation—a process in which sugars are split into carbon dioxide, alcohol or lactic acid, and energy. Very primitive organisms such as yeast engage in fermentation.

Later, **eukaryotes**—more complex cells with a membrane-bound nucleus and a more organized internal structure—developed. As life proliferated, the molecules that these simple organisms absorbed for food became scarce. Because cells could no longer rely on receiving nutrition from the environment, organisms had to evolve the ability to make their own food. Both prokaryotes and eukaryotes evolved **photosynthesis**, the primary way of making food energy on the Earth, about 3.5 billion years ago.

Plants, which are photosynthetic eukaryotes, use carbon dioxide (CO_2) and water (H_2O) to produce sugar ($C_6H_{12}O_6$) and oxygen (O_2). The simplified chemical reaction for photosynthesis is:

$$6CO_2 + 12H_2O + \text{solar energy} = C_6H_{12}O_6 + 6O_2 + 6H_2O$$

Earth's atmosphere contained very little oxygen until the first photosynthetic organisms appeared. Initially, the oxygen bonded with free iron in rocks and seawater to form iron oxide compounds (rust). It was only after all of the exposed free iron was oxidized that oxygen molecules could accumulate in the atmosphere. Once free oxygen was abundant, ozone could form. **Ozone** (O_3) is the form of oxygen in the upper atmosphere that protects the Earth's creatures from the Sun's harmful ultraviolet radiation (UV). More complex biological molecules, which previously would have been broken up by high energy UV, could then evolve. Once oxygen was present in the atmosphere, animals could evolve, too.

Although photosynthesis is by far the greatest source of food energy on the Earth, food energy is also made by organisms that engage in **chemosynthesis**. Chemosynthetic organisms break down chemicals for energy; they are found only at hydrothermal vents. If life originated at hydrothermal vents, then it is likely that chemosynthesis evolved before photosynthesis.

Evolution on the early Earth was very slow. From single-celled organisms evolved multicellular eukaryotes, which appeared about 1 billion years ago when giant mats of algae coated the Earth. (**Algae** are a very diverse group of organisms that photosynthesize, but are not plants.) Multicellular animals evolved about 300 million years later, when plants had produced enough atmospheric oxygen for **respiration**. This process uses oxygen to convert sugar into energy that plants and animals can use and resembles photosynthesis in reverse:

$$C_6H_{12}O_6 + 6O_2 = 6CO_2 + 6H_2O + \text{useable energy}$$

Respiration and photosynthesis are gas exchange processes. In photosynthesis, CO_2 is converted to O_2; in respiration, O_2 is converted to CO_2.

Over enormous amounts of time, many types of creatures evolved from the earliest multicellular organisms.

EVOLUTION BY NATURAL SELECTION

Evolution by natural selection is responsible for the incredible biodiversity found on Earth. **Evolution** means change over time, and the theory of evolution describes how creatures changed over time to adapt to the extraordinary number of **habitats** available to them. A habitat is a type of environment defined by its climate, resource availability, and predators, to name just a few factors. (**Predators** are animals that kill and eat other animals for food.) Habitats occupy such diverse locations as the Arctic, with its constant darkness in winter and constant sunlight in summer; the **desert**, with its relentless sunlight and months-long droughts; and the tropics, where the climate is warm and wet and relatively constant. Each habitat is full of organisms that are uniquely suited for life under those conditions. If the conditions in the habitat change, the species must evolve.

As Charles Darwin (1809–1882), originator of the theory of evolution said, "It is not the strongest of the species that survives, nor the most intelligent that survives. It is the one that is the most adaptable to change."

Natural selection is the mechanism for evolution that Darwin proposed. The naturalist recognized that the world is a dangerous place: There is competition for food, shelter, living space, and mates. Many young organisms are eaten by predators or die in a harsh environment before they reach reproductive age. Because of this, each generation produces more offspring than are needed to replace the parents. The traits of these young organisms are different; some are faster swimmers, or have more camouflaged coloring, or have longer necks or tongues. Because of this (plus a bit of chance), some offspring have an edge over others in the competition for resources and avoidance of predators. These young with an edge are *more likely* to survive to reproduce and pass on their favorable traits to their offspring. The organisms that are less fit for their environment are likely not to survive to reproduce. Over time, the favorable traits are selected for, and the unfavorable traits die out. Natural selection is very much like **artificial selection**, the process by which breeders mate dogs for keen eyesight or soft fur.

How would Darwin have explained how giraffes evolved their long necks? In a population of giraffe ancestors, some had longer necks than others. These animals were able to reach the leaves that were a little higher up on the trees, so they ate more than the many animals that were competing for food closer to the ground. The longer-necked animals were healthier and could have attracted more mates. As a result, the longer-necked animals might have produced more off-spring, and some of these offspring might have had relatively long necks. Over many, many generations, the result would be the giraffe,

The Role of Hypothesis, Theory, and Law in Science

Science has a unique way of looking at how the world works; it is unique because it is based on fact and interpretation rather than on faith. Science provides a system for determining how the world works, known as the **scientific method**. Besides being a way of looking at reality and a process for finding out about it, science is the body of knowledge accumulated by using the scientific method.

The scientific method has a well-defined series of steps. Using background information, a scientist creates a hypothesis to explain an observed phenomenon. The scientist then tests the hypothesis by making observations and performing experiments. The facts determined by observation or experimentation are termed **data** (the singular is *datum*). More than one hypothesis may be present to explain a phenomenon.

If, after further tests, one hypothesis explains all the data while the others do not, and there are no data that contradict that hypothesis, it becomes a **theory**. A theory is supported by many observations, and no major inconsistencies are evident. A theory can also predict behavior. Accepted theories are sometimes overthrown when new opposing data are discovered; but the longer a theory is fundamental to a discipline, the more data it has to back it up, and the more accepted it is. The theory of evolution and the theory of plate tectonics are the frameworks on which their respective fields, biology and geology, are built. They may change in detail, but it seems unlikely that either will be overthrown.

A **law** explains events that occur with unvarying uniformity under a given set of circumstances. The law of gravity explains that an object will fall toward the center of the Earth when dropped—and that it will do so every single time. Theories are explanations that build on physical laws, such as the law of gravity, but they cannot become laws. Although the theory of evolution will never be a law, calling it a theory does not diminish the theory's importance as an explanation of how the world works or diminish its value to science.

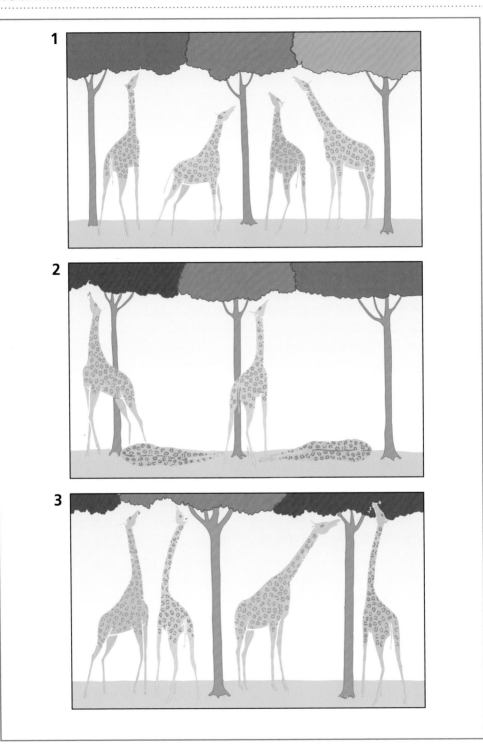

an animal that can eat leaves on trees that no other grazing animals can reach.

Darwin did not know exactly how this occurred because he did not know about **genes**. These units of inheritance were discovered by Gregor Mendel (1822–1884), an Austrian monk who experimented with flower color in pea plants. Mendel discovered that each individual has a gene (he called them factors) that determines a particular trait—for example, flower color. The different forms of a gene for any given trait are **alleles** of that gene: for example, the flower color gene in pea plants might have a red allele and a white allele. These traits do not blend but are passed from parent to offspring as discrete entities; a red-flowering pea plant and a white-flowering pea plant do not have pink-flowering offspring.

In pea plants, red flowers are dominant and white flowers are recessive, meaning that if an offspring receives one red flower allele and one white flower allele from its parents, it will have red flowers (the red flower allele is expressed). A pea plant will only have white flowers if it has two white flower alleles, one from each of its parents. So in one generation, most pea plants may have red flowers, but if it becomes advantageous for pea plants to have white flowers, those with white flowers will survive to reproduce and pass their white-flower genes on to the next generation. In time, most of the pea plants will have white flowers. In this way, a recessive trait gives the species the flexibility to survive if conditions change.

British scientist Charles Darwin introduced the theory of natural selection in his 1859 book *The Origin of Species by Means of Natural Selection*. His theory suggests that certain organisms within species thrive while weaker members die or do not successfully reproduce. The thriving organisms then pass their favorable traits to their offspring and over time, the species changes, or evolves. The giraffes here are examples: the shorter giraffes die of malnourishment because they cannot reach the leaves. The longer-necked giraffes pass their genes to their offspring and therefore the species becomes more fit for survival.

Besides the diversity of alleles that are found in a population, an allele may change so that it produces a different variation of a trait (for example, green flowers in pea plants) by a process called **mutation**. Exposure to UV or certain chemicals may cause a mutation, or a mutation may have no cause. Mutations are random; they have no purpose, and most are either neutral or harmful. Occasionally, a mutation is helpful, and the introduction of that allele into the **gene pool** (all of the alleles available in the genetic makeup of a population) gives the species a trait that helps it to adapt to its environment.

If the environment an organism lives in changes and causes different alleles to be expressed, the species will evolve into a different species. The biologist's way of defining evolution is a change in allele frequency over time. A new species arises through a process known as **speciation**. This process most often happens when a relatively small number of individuals of a parent species (Species A) are separated from the rest of the population. The environments they live in and the alleles present within the two groups may be somewhat different; thus, over time a new species (Species B) evolves. If Species B comes back into contact with Species A, and Species B is better adapted to the environment, Species B may produce more offspring that survive to reproduce than Species A. Ultimately, Species A may undergo **extinction**. An organism becomes extinct when it no longer produces enough young to replace itself. The end may come very slowly or very rapidly.

Charles Darwin observed the results of speciation in finches on different islands of the Galapagos. Each island was home to a species of finch with a differently shaped bill, depending on the types of food that were widely available on the island. The distances between the islands kept the populations separate. Darwin hypothesized, and it has since been proved by DNA analysis, that a single ancestor finch species was the parent stock (likely blown by wind to the islands from the South American mainland). From that single species, finches were blown to the different islands, where their isolation allowed them to evolve into 14 different species, 13 on the Galapagos and one on Cocos Island.

Horses evolved in response to a changing environment. Horse ancestors were fox-sized creatures that lived in forests about 55 million years ago (MYA). As climate changed, vast forests gave way to grasslands. The horse ancestors became taller and grew longer legs to see over the grass, reduced the number of toes to form a hoof suited for walking in grassland, and evolved longer teeth with complex enamel to be able to chew grasses that contain hard silica. These trends continued over tens of millions of years until the emergence of the modern horse about 2 MYA.

The theory of evolution has an enormous amount of scientific evidence to support it. Darwin amassed some of this evidence, but some has come to light with advances in scientific knowledge in the decades since. The fundamental concept is that all life forms are related; more closely related organisms are more similar to each other than more distantly related organisms. The evidence that supports the theory of evolution includes:

- All life forms are composed of the same chemical elements, mostly carbon, nitrogen, hydrogen, and oxygen.
- The chromosomes of all organisms are composed of DNA, except bacteria, which have RNA.
- Proteins are synthesized the same way in all cells.
- The development of an **embryo**, the early stage of an organism before it is born, retraces that organism's evolutionary history. Embryonic development is more similar in organisms that are more closely related. Fish, chimps, and humans look very similar in their earliest stages; but soon thereafter, fish begin to look different. Chimps and humans look similar until very late in their development, suggesting that chimps and humans are more closely related to each other than either chimps or humans are to fish.
- The forelimbs of humans, whales, dogs, and birds are composed of the same types of bones and have similar arrangement of muscles, nerves, and blood vessels. These are **homologous structures**, which are different structures

that appear as if they were modified from the same starting material.

- Many "missing links" have been found in the fossil record. Fossils showing the gradation from a reptilelike jaw connection to a mammal-like jaw have been discovered in South America, for example.

- Although no one has witnessed the evolution of one species into another, small evolutionary changes occur all the time. Insects evolve resistance to pesticides and bacteria to antibiotics. The alleles for resistance existed within or mutated into the organisms' gene pool and allowed them to adapt to an environment that now includes pesticides and antibiotics.

- Nonfunctional, or partly functional, remnants of organs and structures that are no longer useful and are being lost are **vestigial structures**. Dogs have dewclaws. They walk on four toes; but the fifth digit, located higher on the animal's leg, serves no purpose. In one group of toothless whales, a full set of teeth grows in the embryos but is reabsorbed before birth. Internally, humans have tail structures, and snakes have leg structures.

One of the great thinkers on modern evolutionary theory, Stephen Jay Gould (1941–2002), often said that evolution is not seen in perfection; it is seen in mistakes. The human back is a good example. Human ancestors walked on all fours, and the back was well adapted for horizontal posture. When humans began to walk upright, evolutionary processes, over a period of many thousands of years, modified those structures for an entirely different orientation. The spine, which had functioned structurally as a beam, was now a pillar with the discs poorly placed. The spine had to support and balance more body weight, including much of the torso and the head, since the forelimbs no longer provided support or bore weight. Gould pointed to the human back as an example of a structure that would have been much better had it been designed from scratch rather than being a modified piece of equipment, as the number of adults with back problems suggests.

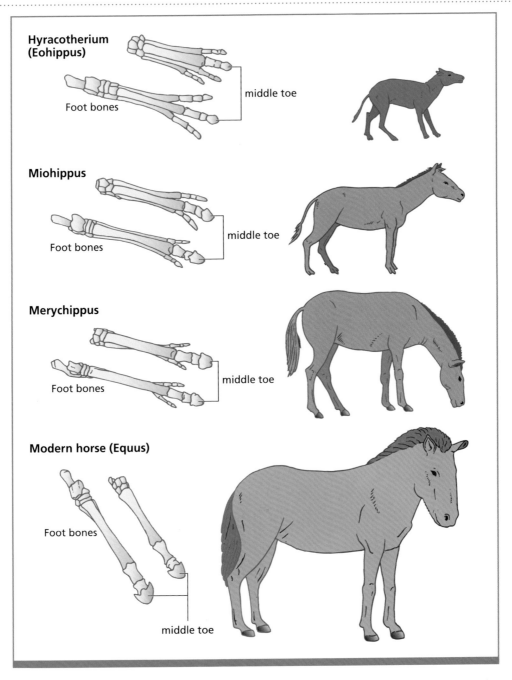

Hyracotherium (Eohippus)

Foot bones

middle toe

Miohippus

Foot bones

middle toe

Merychippus

Foot bones

middle toe

Modern horse (Equus)

Foot bones

middle toe

Evolution is easily seen in the fossil record left by horses. As forests evolved into grasslands, horses became taller so that they could see over the grass and evolved hooves that could move swiftly through the grass. Their teeth also became better adapted for chewing grasses.

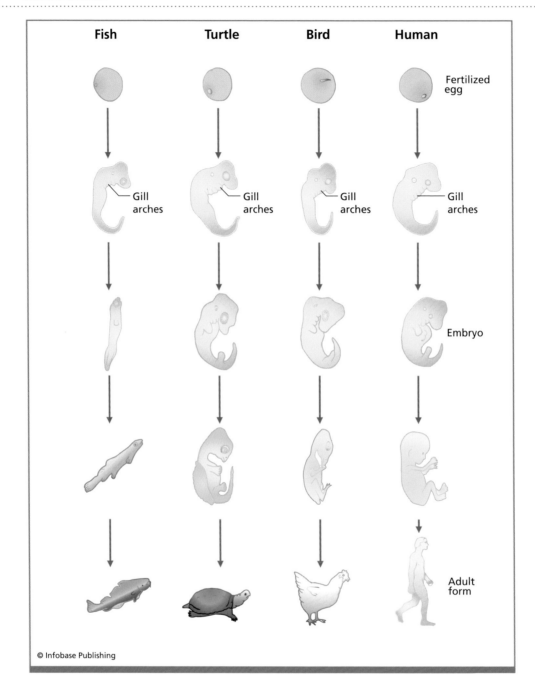

Evidence for evolution includes the similarities in the early development of vertebrate embryos. All of the embryos appear very similar and even have gill arches, although most terrestrial vertebrates do not have gills. These gill arches are remnants from an evolutionary ancestor that lived in an aquatic environment.

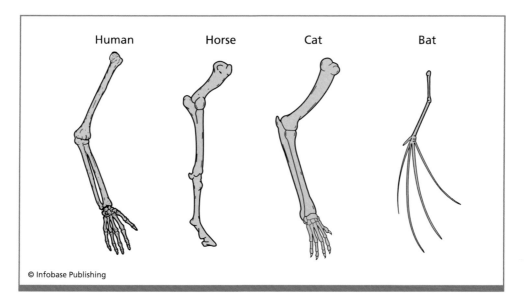

Human   Horse   Cat   Bat

© Infobase Publishing

Evidence for evolution includes the similarity in structure of vertebrate forelimbs. Although humans, horses, cats, and bats engage in very different activities with their forelimbs, the bones that make up those limbs are the same; they are just present in very different proportions.

Evolution has no goal; there is no pinnacle. Evolutionary success could be measured by the amount of time a species has survived on the Earth, by the number of species or individuals that are present, or by the number of niches a group of organisms fills. (A **niche** is the position or function of an organism in its community of plants and animals.) Coelacanths have lived in the deep sea, more or less unchanged, for hundreds of millions of years. Are they the most successful organisms on Earth? Insects far outnumber other types of organisms. Are insects more successful than coelacanths? Numerous species of dinosaurs filled nearly every niche on the planet for 165 million years until they all went extinct. Does their extinction negate that they were exquisitely evolved organisms for the conditions of the Mesozoic Era? Or are humans, the only organisms that can substantially modify the environment to suit their needs, the pinnacle of evolution even though our species has been around for only 200,000 years?

GEOLOGIC TIME

Evolution does not take place on a human timescale—in days, years, decades, or even centuries. Great amounts of time are needed for natural selection to change the genes in a population enough for a new species to evolve. To better deal with the large expanse of time since the Earth formed, scientists have created the geologic timescale. The units on the geologic timescale are bounded by important events, such as major changes in climate or **mass extinctions**—events in which enormous numbers of species go extinct during a fairly short period. These timescale units are given names, and events that occurred during those time periods are referred to by those names. The Cambrian period began 540 MYA, when life on Earth suddenly became abundant for example. The Cretaceous-Tertiary boundary falls at the time, 66 MYA, when the dinosaurs and many other organisms went extinct. The **Pleistocene** period, between 2 million and 10,000 years ago, corresponds with the most recent Ice Ages. Some people say that Earth now is in an interglacial period within the Pleistocene; others say that we have moved on to a different time period, which is referred to as the Holocene.

BIODIVERSITY

There are three types of biodiversity:

- *Genetic diversity* is the number of alleles of a single gene that are present in a species' gene pool. If the genetic diversity is too small, a species may not be able to evolve to adapt to a changing environment.
- About 13 million species of microbes, plants, and animals represent the planet's *species diversity*, although only 1.75 million species have been identified. Many of the unknown species are insects of the tropical rain forests that are very difficult to find and catalog. Some of the unknown species, though, are fish, reptiles, birds, and mammals that live in obscure places.

⊕   The wide variety of the Earth's **ecosystems**, or its *ecosystem diversity*, provide habitat for the enormous number of species found on the planet.

The term *biodiversity* describes a region's variety of life. For most types of organisms, biodiversity is highest in the tropics, where the climate is favorable, and lowest toward the poles, where the day length variation is extreme and the climate is harsh. The more differences there are in an environment, the greater its biodiversity will be because it will have more niches. On land, temperature, precipitation, soil type, and other factors determine a location's diversity. In the oceans, temperature, salinity, pressure, and other factors create subenvironments that allow different species to exist.

Much of the world's biodiversity is found on islands. A species of organism migrates to an island and then evolves to meet the requirements of the new environment. If conditions are different enough from its original habitat, the organism will evolve into a new species, as in the case of Darwin's finches, known as an **endemic species**. A species that is endemic to a location cannot be found anywhere else.

WRAP-UP

Using the scientific method, biologists have developed the theory of evolution by natural selection. As the environment changes, one species may evolve into other species as more favorable traits are selected for and less favorable traits are eliminated. Species that cannot adapt to a changing environment may go extinct. These mechanisms, taking place over roughly 4 billion years, have allowed living organisms to adapt to the myriad habitats found on the Earth and have resulted in the planet's remarkable biodiversity.

Life on Earth

A very detailed and thorough classification system has been developed in an effort to categorize all of Earth's varied life forms. Scientists classify every living creature with a two-part **scientific name** representing the organism's genus and species. Organisms that are in the same species are the most closely related; those of different species but in the same genus are somewhat less closely related. The classification system continues on to broader categories of family, order, class, and phylum, until finally it reaches the broadest category: kingdom. Earth's organisms are divided into five kingdoms (see the table on page 21). The most visible are the members of the plant and animal kingdoms, which account for most of the biodiversity that people can see.

SCIENTIFIC CLASSIFICATION

The current classification system was developed by Swedish naturalist Carolus Linnaeus (1707–1778), who based his classification on an organism's anatomical structures. Modern scientists augment Linnaeus's original structural categories with DNA analyses. Linnaeus's system delineated seven categories, from the broadest to the most specific: Kingdom, phylum, class, order, family, genus, and species. The scientific name of an organism is its genus and species names. For example, *Canus* is the genus of all doglike creatures; it includes the species *lupus* (wolves); *latrans* (coyotes); and *familiaris* (domestic dogs). The only category that is meaningful in nature is the species; the rest are constructs that people use to better understand their world.

The seven classification categories may also have subgroups, super groups, and infra groups. Examples include subkingdom, superfamily, and infraclass. The same table on page 21 shows the two broadest categories of living organisms, superkingdom and kingdom. Organisms are ordinarily referred to by genus and species, but if it is necessary to be more specific, a subspecies name is included. For example,

Earth's Kingdoms

SUPERKINGDOM PROKARYOTA	SUPERKINGDOM EUKARYOTA
Kingdom Monera: bacteria, archaebacteria, and blue-green algae	Kingdom Protista: algae (other than blue-green algae), protozoa, and slime molds
	Kingdom Fungi: fungi
	Kingdom Plantae: plants, including mosses, liverworts, hornworts, whisk ferns, club mosses, horsetails, ferns, cycads, conifers, gnetophytes, ginkgophytes, and flowering plants
	Kingdom Animalia: animals, including **invertebrates** (animals without backbones) and **vertebrates** (animals with backbones)

Strix occidentalis caurina distinguishes the Northern Spotted Owl from spotted owls in other regions.

VIRUSES AND BACTERIA

Viruses barely meet the criteria for life: among their unusual features, they must invade and control the cells of other organisms to reproduce. For this reason, all viruses are **parasites**, organisms that obtain nourishment from a host and may cause illness in that host. Viruses are not included in any kingdom.

Members of the Kingdom Monera—bacteria, archaebacteria, and blue-green algae—are the smallest, most diverse, and among the most abundant living organisms: 34 ounces (1 liter) of seawater can contain 2.5 billion bacteria; 0.04 ounces (1 gram) of fertile soil may hold up to 100 million bacteria. Members of the Kingdom Monera are found in nearly all conditions: in the bodies of living organisms, in the ocean floor, in frozen ice caps and hot springs, and even in the upper atmosphere.

Some bacteria engage in photosynthesis or chemosynthesis; they are **primary producers** (organisms that produce food energy from inorganic materials). Many more are **consumers** (organisms that depend on other living creatures for their food energy). The most important role of bacteria is as **decomposers**; they break down dead plant and animal tissue and waste products into nutrients, which are used by plants to make food. **Nutrients** are biologically important ions that are critical to plant cell growth (nitrogen and phosphorous); for building shells and skeletons (silica and calcium); and for the production of proteins and other biochemicals (nitrates and phosphates).

Most bacteria are **aerobic**, meaning they breathe oxygen. **Anaerobic** bacteria live in oxygen-poor environments and break down compounds such as sulfate to get oxygen. Without anaerobic bacteria, the organic material that fell into oxygen-poor waters in sea or lake bottoms would not decompose, and those nutrients would be lost. A few bacteria are **pathogens** that bring about diseases in plants and animals, including tuberculosis, syphilis, and cholera in humans.

PROTISTS AND FUNGI

Kingdom Protista is made of eukaryotic organisms that do not fit into another kingdom. The most important are **phytoplankton,** microscopic algae that are ubiquitous in surface waters in oceans and lakes and that are responsible for about 50% of the world's **primary productivity** (the food energy created by producers). **Fungi** include yeasts, molds, and mushrooms, all of which absorb nutrients from living or dead plant or animal tissues. Many fungi are important decomposers, although some are parasites, such as those that cause ringworm and athlete's foot. Although some species of mushrooms are farmed for food, and others are used to produce industrial chemicals such as lactic acid, hundreds of mushroom species are toxic.

PLANTS

Members of Kingdom Plantae are eukaryotic and multicellular. The roughly 300,000 species mostly photosynthesize, although about 300 species are parasites. Plants are rooted to the ground, with cellulose in their cell walls to give them a rigid body structure.

Vascular plants have roots, stems, and leaves for transporting water and food and a cuticle that helps them resist drying out. Seeds, with their hard coating, protect the embryo. Because of these features, vascular plants colonize many land environments. **Gymnosperms** are woody, perennial, vascular plants, mostly cone-bearing (coniferous) trees that are common in many environments. The reproductive organs of flowering plants, or **angiosperms,** are found in their flowers, and their seeds are encased in a fruit. Angiosperms are found wherever plant life is possible, even in shallow fresh and saline (salty) water.

Plants are the source of food energy for nearly all animals, and they produce oxygen, the essential gas. People use plants for wood, fibers, pharmaceuticals, oils, latex, pigments, and resins. Ancient plants form **fossil fuels,** such as petroleum and coal, which are the most important energy source for modern society. Fossil fuels are **hydrocarbons**, organic compounds composed of hydrogen and carbon.

ANIMALS

All animals are multicellular and do not create their own food energy. Most have muscle cells so they can move, and a nervous system and sense organs so they can sense and respond to their environment. These adaptations help animals obtain food. Most animals have a digestive system, and most reproduce sexually.

Invertebrates

Invertebrates lack a backbone, although many have an external skeleton for protection, to keep from drying out, and to give them a supporting structure. Approximately 95% of all animal species are invertebrates, most of them insects. For every individual vertebrate, there are 200 million invertebrates. In the oceans, invertebrates fill every microhabitat. Tiny floating **zooplankton**, for example, consume phytoplankton and are an extremely important food source for higher marine animals.

Worms obtain food by stripping mud of its organic matter or as parasites. **Mollusks**, which include snails, clams, squid, and octopuses, have an external or internal shell for protection from the elements and predators. Most of the 44,000 species of **crustaceans**, including crabs, lobsters, and shrimp, live in the oceans. **Echinoderms**—sea stars, brittle stars, sea urchins, sand dollars, and sea cucumbers—cling to the seafloor at all ocean depths and in nearly all water temperatures.

More than one million species of **arthropods** are known, and about 90% of them are insects, including beetles; moths and butterflies; wasps, ants, and bees; flies and mosquitoes; grasshoppers and crickets; and cockroaches. The enormous evolutionary success of the insects is attributed to their small size, high reproductive rate, and ability to adapt rapidly to environmental changes. These small creatures inhabit nearly every ecosystem except the polar regions and the oceans. Insects eat plants or decaying tissue or prey on insects or other small animals; some are parasites. Insects may attack crops or carry diseases. But many are beneficial: They consume harmful

A swallowtail butterfly (*Papilio sp.*) alights on spring flowers. *(Tom Coleman, University of Kentucky / USDA Forest Service)*

insects; scavenge for dead tissue; break up soil to allow air in; pollinate plants; and provide people with food, honey, beeswax, silk, and other substances.

Vertebrates

Vertebrates are much more similar to each other than are invertebrates. Because of their skeletal support, vertebrates can be relatively large. Most have two pairs of appendages: fins, limbs, or wings. Fish, amphibians, and reptiles are **ectotherms**, with body temperatures the same as the surrounding environment. These "cold-blooded" animals are adapted to a specific range of temperatures: Tropical fish and most reptiles live only in warm climates, while amphibians and cold-water fish live in cooler climates. Birds and mammals are **endotherms**.

These "warm-blooded" animals keep their body temperatures nearly constant, independent of the temperature of their surroundings. Endotherms keep warm by consuming large amounts of food, and they maintain their body temperature with insulation: feathers, fur, or blubber. Endotherms can tolerate a large temperature range and can live in a wide variety of environments.

Earth is home to nearly 50,000 species of vertebrates in seven classes:

- Agnatha, Chondrichthyes, Osteichthyes (fish): These three classes are ectothermic, aquatic vertebrates with gills, usually fins, and an elongated body covered with scales.
- Amphibia (amphibian): Ectothermic vertebrates with aquatic larvae; adults live in land or water; the class includes frogs, toads, newts, salamanders, and caecilians
- Reptilia (reptiles): Egg-laying ectothermic vertebrates with scaly, dry skin. Reptiles can live away from water because of their skin and hard-shelled eggs
- Aves (birds): Endothermic, egg-laying vertebrates with feathers for insulation; most fly
- Mammalia (mammals): Endothermic vertebrates that are covered with hair or fur for insulation, nourish their young with milk from the mammary glands, and mostly give live birth to young.

Fish

Fish live in fresh or salt water of all depths and all temperatures, although they are more abundant in surface and coastal waters where food is more common. Fish breathe through gills, which extract oxygen from water and pass CO_2 back into water.

Cartilaginous fish (class Chondrichthyes), primarily consisting of sharks, are extremely diverse and successful; they have remained nearly unchanged for 70 million years. Sharks feed on fish and invertebrates, and large sharks may even eat marine mammals. Bony fish (class Osteichthyes) are even more plentiful and diverse. Streamlined fish, such as tuna and mackerel, are predators that move swiftly through the water in search of small prey. Flatfish, including sole and halibut, peer up from their protected positions on the seafloor. Elongate fish, such as eels, squeeze into spaces between and under rocks. Fins allow fish to push themselves through the water and also to turn, brake, and balance. Flying fish use their fins to glide above the sea surface, and mudskippers walk on their fins. Most fish travel in schools ranging in size from a few fish to groups that cover several square miles.

Amphibians

Amphibians need to live in or near water, since neither the adults nor the eggs can maintain their water content like higher animals can. Members of the order Caudata (salamanders and newts) have long tails and equal-sized front and rear legs, similar to lizards. Members of the order Anura (frogs and toads) have large, muscular hind legs for jumping, webbed feet for swimming, and no tail. Frogs absorb oxygen dissolved in water when they are in wet places and breathe less efficiently through lungs when they are not. Most frogs eat insects and worms, although some large tropical species eat small mammals and snakes. Toads have stouter bodies and thicker skins, allowing them to live farther from water.

Reptiles

Reptiles are scaly, dry-skinned, air breathers. Their lungs, waterproof skin, and shelled eggs allow them to live away from water. These ectotherms move between sun and shade to keep their body temperature as close to optimal as possible. Most reptiles live on tropical and subtropical land; a few live in warm waters. The two most visible orders of reptiles include Crocodilia (crocodiles, caimans, and alligators), Squamata (lizards and snakes), and Testudines (turtles). Lizards have low bodies, long tails, and legs that extend outward from the sides of their bodies. Snakes (and legless lizards) have no limbs.

Turtles have a shell for protection. Dinosaurs (superorder Dinosauria) are perhaps the most famous reptiles, and they have been extinct for 65 million years (except for those that evolved into birds).

Birds

Because birds are endotherms with feathers for insulation and hard-shelled eggs, they can live in a wide range of environments and therefore are the most diverse class of terrestrial vertebrates. Birds eat insects, seeds, fruit, fish, small mammals, and carrion (dead animals). Species range in size from tiny hummingbirds (order Trochiliformes) to enormous ostriches (order Struthioniformes).

Most birds can fly, although a few have lost the ability and have developed other adaptations such as running (ostriches) or swimming (penguins). Flying birds are lightweight, with a bony bill rather than

Blue-footed booby, North Seymour Island, Ecuador. *(© Jeff Greenberg / The Image Works)*

heavy jaws and teeth, and hollow but strong bony skeletons. Flight allows birds to migrate so that they can be in a favorable environment year round. Bird bills are adapted for a particular type of food: They can be long and thin for sucking nectar from flowers, large and strong for cracking seeds, or sharp and deadly for hunting and consuming rodents. Seabirds may have webbed feet for swimming; long legs for wading; fat deposits, light bones, and air sacs for buoyancy; an oily secretion for waterproofing feathers and providing insulation; highly developed eyesight for locating fish in the water; and a salt gland over the eye to eliminate excess salt.

Mammals

Mammals are air-breathing endotherms with hair or fur for insulation that allows them to live in nearly all environments; although most of the 5,500 species are terrestrial, a few are aquatic. Mammals are born from their mother's body and fed mother's milk when they are young.

The majority of mammals are placental: The fetus is nourished by a uterine placenta, and the young are born fully developed. Roughly half of all mammal species are in the order Rodentia; rodents range in size from the African Pygmy Mouse, at 2.4 inches (6 centimeters) long and 0.25 ounces (7 grams) in weight, to the South American Capybara, which weighs 100 pounds (45 kilograms). Rodents reproduce rapidly and are good food sources for larger animals. They spread seeds and also diseases: The Black Plague pandemic of the mid-fourteenth century, which killed about one-third of Europe's population, was spread by black rats. Bats (order Chiroptera) are the only true flying mammals. Most eat insects, but some consume fruit, fish, rodents, or even other bats. Fruit bats are important for spreading seeds.

Members of the order Carnivora include 260 species of flesh-eating mammals, such as cats, dogs, mongooses, bears, seals, and walrus. Order Insectivora includes small animals such as shrews and moles. The two orders of hoofed mammals are the odd-toed Perissodactyla, which includes the horse and rhinoceros, and the even-toed Artiodactyla, which includes the deer, antelope, camel, pig, and cow.

Whales, dolphins, and porpoises (order Cetacea) are marine mammals. **Cetaceans** have streamlined bodies, slippery skin or sleek hair, and limbs that allow swimming rather than walking. They are intelligent, with complex family and social groupings. To live in the cold water, cetaceans have a high metabolic rate, a large surface area-to-volume ratio, capillaries in their skin to reduce heat loss, and layers of fat and fur for insulation.

Humans, monkeys, apes, and lemurs belong to the order Primates, characterized by hands with opposing thumbs, short fingernails (no claws), long, inward-closing fingers, and binocular vision. Monkeys are divided into two main types: New World Monkeys, including the appealing capuchin and spider monkeys of the South American forests, and Old World Monkeys, such as the baboons and macaques of Africa and Eurasia. Great apes, from the family Hominidae, include humans, chimpanzees, gorillas, and orangutans. Humans, chimps, and gorillas are members of the subfamily Homininae. Common chimps (*Pan troglodytes*) and humans (*Homo sapiens*) share about 98% of their DNA, making them such close relatives that some scientists have suggested that the common chimp be admitted to the genus *Homo* (*Homo troglodytes)* or that humans be placed in genus *Pan* (*Pan sapiens*).

With intelligence as an adaptive strategy, humans have colonized nearly every habitat on the land, from the coldest polar regions to the steamiest tropical jungles. Unlike other animals that can only make small changes, humans can alter their environment until it is unrecognizable (e.g., Tokyo) to suit their needs and desires.

WRAP-UP

Nearly every microenvironment on Earth has some form of life adapted to it. The incredible diversity of these habitats has resulted in an equally amazing array of organisms to inhabit them. From the simplest virus and the extremely primitive shark, to the communicative and intelligent dolphin or human, life has evolved all sorts of ways to fill its needs and to leave behind offspring. But organisms do not live in isolation from other species or from their environment; their organization into ecosystems is described in the following chapter.

Earth's Ecosystems

Plants, animals, and other life forms on the Earth live together in ecosystems. Ecosystems occur on many scales; they can be as small as a flea's intestines or as large as the Amazon basin. The entire Earth is also an ecosystem. Ecosystems, therefore, can be nested inside each other. **Biomes** encompass all of the ecosystems that have similar climate and organisms. Tropical rain forests have the most biodiversity of any terrestrial biome, and coral reefs are the most diverse of any ocean ecosystem. Ecosystems provide services to the planet and all of its inhabitants.

FOOD CHAINS AND FOOD WEBS

Ecology is the study of the distribution and abundance of species and their relationship to their environments. One of the primary concerns of ecologists is how food energy is passed from organisms at one **trophic level**—or energy level—to organisms at the next trophic level. This passing of energy is described as the **food chain**.

At the base of every food chain—the first trophic level—are primary producers, mostly photosynthesizers. The second trophic level is inhabited by primary consumers or **herbivores**, the plant-eating animals. The third trophic level is inhabited by the first-level **carnivores**, the animals that eat the herbivores. At the end of all food chains—usually at the third, fourth, fifth, or sixth trophic levels—are the top carnivores, those who eat one or more of the organisms in underlying trophic levels but who are not themselves food for predators. **Scavengers** such as vultures consume plant or animal tissue that is already dead.

Food chains are short because about 90% of the energy consumed is not passed to the next trophic level but stays with the individuals who consume the food. They use the energy for locomotion, reproduction, and the other activities required for daily living. The higher an organism is on the food chain, the more prey it must consume to get enough energy to meet its requirements, the more difficult it is to gather so many prey, and the smaller its population will be. Top carnivores, therefore, are fairly rare and must cover a wide area to meet their nutritional needs.

Although energy can only travel up a food chain, nutrients and water are recycled to all trophic levels. The breakdown of a dead organisms' tissue or excrement, where nutrients and water are stored, requires decomposers such as bacteria and fungi. Without decomposers, each food chain would be only a one-way street, and life on the Earth would have ended soon after it began.

The food-chain model implies that all organisms eat from only one trophic level; but many, including humans, eat from more than one. Therefore, the interactions between organisms are better described as a **food web**. Food webs can be simple, with only a few species interacting, or they can be as complicated as a tropical rain forest, where thousands of species are involved.

A change in the population size of one species in a food web affects other species in the web. For example, if a species at the third trophic level decreases in population or dies out, other species at that trophic level will have more predators after them, but they will

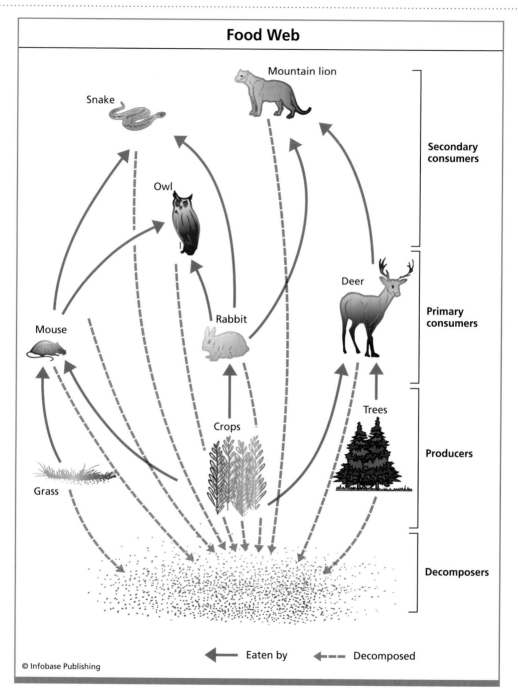

Food Web

Mountain lion

Snake

Owl

Mouse

Rabbit

Deer

Crops

Trees

Grass

Secondary consumers

Primary consumers

Producers

Decomposers

← Eaten by   ◄--- Decomposed

© Infobase Publishing

The interconnections of organisms in a food web are complicated, with some organisms eating from or being eaten by organisms at different tropic levels.

also have more prey available to them. How this plays out depends on many factors, including the specific species involved. The food web will not collapse from the loss of one species unless that organism is a **keystone species**, named for the top center block in a stone arch that holds the other blocks in place. If the keystone is removed, the arch falls. A keystone species is often the top carnivore; but it can also be a predator that keeps prey animal populations from growing too high; a large herbivore that keeps plant life in balance; or a plant that supports insects that serve as food for birds, bats, and other organisms.

An example of a keystone species is the sea otter, which is important to the offshore kelp forest ecosystem. (**Kelp** are fast-growing seaweeds that live in submerged forests near the ocean shore.) Otters feed and play in the kelp forests, where they dine on sea urchins, their favorite food. When sea otters were hunted for their fur, which caused their population to decline precipitously, sea urchins destroyed the kelp forests by eating the holdfasts that attach the seaweeds to the ground. The kelp then washed away, and the forest was destroyed, leaving important fish and shellfish species (including commercially important ones) homeless. Other keystone species include the gray wolf, sea stars, prairie dogs, and the northern spotted owl.

THE MAJOR BIOMES

A biome is a large geographical region with a distinctive climate. Different portions of a biome may be geographically separate, but its plants, animals, and microorganisms will have similar adaptations because they have similar advantages and challenges to meet. Grazing animals of the prairie biome, for example, are fast moving and are adapted for eating grass.

Terrestrial climate zones are defined primarily by temperature, with warmer temperatures occurring at lower latitudes closer to the equator and cooler temperatures occurring at higher latitudes nearer the poles. Where precipitation falls depends partly on latitude—rainfall

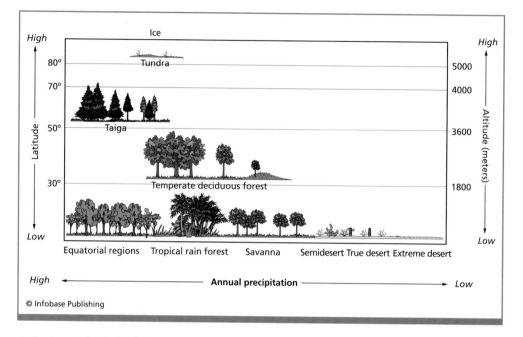

Altitude mimics latitude in temperature and precipitation so ecosystems that are found in polar regions resemble those found on tops of high mountains.

is abundant near the equator and scarce near 30°N and 30°S—and also on the geography of a continent, with coastal areas wetter than interior regions. For example, at around 30°N, New Orleans, Louisiana, receives 57 inches (145 cm) of rainfall annually due to its position near the Gulf of Mexico. However, Tucson, Arizona, located at the same latitude but in an inland desert area, only receives 12 inches (30 cm).

Altitude mimics latitude in biome distribution. Lower elevations are dominated by lower latitude biomes, such as desert or tropical, and higher elevations have higher latitude biomes. A short, 45-mile (72 km) trip from the top of Humphreys Peak, the highest point in Arizona, to the Sonoran Desert below goes from tundra, down through the coniferous forest in the mountains, to the scrub brush of middle elevations, and finally into the hot desert.

Discussed below are some of the major biomes found on planet Earth. This survey begins in the polar regions and moves toward the equator.

Tundra

Near the poles, the Sun is absent or low on the horizon much of the year. The average temperature is 23°F (-5°C), and water within and on the surface of the soil is almost always frozen. To avoid wind and frigid temperatures, plants grow small and close to the ground. This biome is known as **tundra**.

During the cold, dark winters, plants go dormant. Animals hibernate, migrate to more hospitable climes, or struggle to survive. During the summer, days turn long and plants grow rapidly. Insects flourish and birds and large mammals come out of hibernation or migrate back to the region. But with a growing season of only 50 to 60 days, annual productivity is low. The tundra biome has low species diversity since few organisms have been able to adapt to its harsh climatic conditions. Nonetheless, it has very distinctive large mammals including polar bears, caribou, wolves, and musk oxen, and numerous small mammals, such as shrews, squirrels, foxes, and hares. The unusual birds include snowy owls, ptarmigan, and Arctic terns.

Boreal Forest

The largest terrestrial biome is the **boreal forest**, which stretches across Canada and northern Eurasia. Here, the growing season is only 130 days long, and winters are long, cold, and dry. Most precipitation falls as snow, between 16 and 40 inches (40 and 100 cm) each year. The dominant trees are firs, with tough needle-shaped leaves that shed in the winter and can survive frosts. Like the tundra, boreal forests have low species diversity. Mammals include bighorn sheep, Siberian tigers, Canadian lynx, moose, elk, deer, and smaller bats, beavers, raccoon, pikas, lemmings, and shrews; birds of prey include golden eagles, bald eagles, and many types of hawks. Canada's boreal forest is incredibly important for the 3 billion North American songbirds that nest there each summer.

Temperate Forest

Temperate forests are found across North America and Eurasia in cool climates where annual rainfall is high. The long growing season results in high primary productivity. The uppermost layer of the forest is the **canopy**, which is formed by the tops of the main body of trees. Unlike tropical forests, light penetrates to the forest floor, and plants grow on and near the ground. Animals may inhabit a three-dimensional world: on the ground or in the soil, in low shrubs or small trees, or high in the forest canopy.

The two types of temperate forest are adapted to the two distinct climates of the temperate latitudes. **Deciduous** forests are found where summers are hot and winters are cold. Deciduous trees typically have broad leaves with a wide surface for photosynthesizing in the summer, but they lose these leaves in winter so that they do not freeze. Animals in this biome include black bears, deer, wolf, fox, eagles, and small mammals such as squirrels, martins, and rabbits. At one time, deciduous forests covered Europe, the eastern United States, and some parts of Asia, but most have been logged and the land converted to farmland.

The trees of **evergreen** forests are found where both summers and winters are mild. Thus, the trees do not lose their leaves or needles seasonally. The western United States and Canada are home to spectacular evergreen forests of giant redwoods and Douglas fir, which can grow up to 400 feet (120 m) tall. Bald eagles, peregrine falcons, and northern spotted owls nest in the canopy, while black bears, black-tailed deer, and rabbits live on the forest floor. Evergreen trees are highly valued for their lumber, and many of these forests have disappeared.

Old-growth forests have never been logged or have not been logged for hundreds of years. Old-growth forests are very rich ecosystems because they include young trees, old trees, standing dead trees, and decaying logs that provide a myriad of habitats for wildlife. Important old-growth forests include the grand Douglas fir, western hemlock, giant sequoia, and coastal redwood forests of the western

United States, the loblolly pine forests of the southeastern United States, the boreal forests of Canada, and tropical rain forests.

Prairie and Grassland

Prairies and grasslands are found at similar latitudes to temperate forests, but here the climate is harsher and drier. Plants are drought tolerant and low to the ground to help them survive strong winds. Grazing and burrowing animals, such as badgers and prairie dogs, are dominant. Large herd animals roam these prairies: kangaroos and wallabies in Australia; zebra, antelopes, and giraffe in the African veldt, and bison and pronghorn antelope in North America. Lions, cougars, wolves, eagles, and other predators keep the numbers of these animals in check, but human hunters have reduced or

Migrating baboons on the African savannah in Kenya. *(Kenneth M. Gale / USDA Forest Service)*

eliminated predator populations worldwide. Grassland soils are very rich, and these regions are now extensively farmed and grazed by domesticated animals.

Chaparral

The chaparral biome has mild, wet winters and long, dry summers. Chaparral plants survive this drought period by having small, hard leaves that limit the amount of water they lose and by having both deep and shallow roots that help them to gather as much water as possible. Coyotes, jackrabbits, foxes, skunks, and snakes frequent these regions. This biome is found along the California coast, and in Israel, South Africa, and Australia. Today, many of these regions have been overgrazed or urbanized. It is now believed that agriculture originated in the chaparral zone in Iraq.

The Importance of Fire in Ecosystems

Fires, which start naturally from lightning strikes or spontaneous combustion of dry vegetation, are important to many ecosystems. Because fire is an unavoidable element of most arid environments, many organisms have adapted to it or even need it for their survival. For example, some trees have seeds that germinate only after a fire. In the pine barrens of the southeastern United States, fire clears out small trees such as hickories and oaks, giving the more fire-resistant pines space to grow. Similarly, fire maintains grassland by keeping out the trees that try to colonize the area.

Fires burn the leaves and other organic matter that collects on the forest floor. If fires are suppressed, too much of this material accumulates so that when the inevitable fire comes, it burns hotter and covers a larger area. With more fuel, the fire travels up the tree trunks, damaging leaves and wood. An intense fire may even burn the organic portion of the topsoil, making recovery of the ecosystem difficult. In many regions, forest management strategies include controlled burning to keep down the accumulation of fuel.

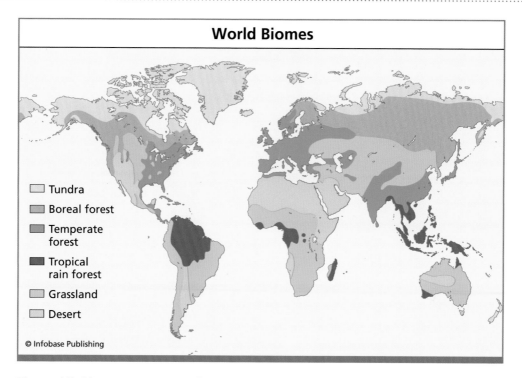

World Biomes

- Tundra
- Boreal forest
- Temperate forest
- Tropical rain forest
- Grassland
- Desert

© Infobase Publishing

The world's biomes encompass all of the similar ecosystems that are found in regions with similar climate conditions. Only the major biomes are shown in this diagram.

Desert

Deserts cover up to one-third of the planet's land surface. They are most common at latitudes 30°N and 30°S of the equator, where warm, dry air descends, although they also occur in the rain shadow on the leeward side of mountains. Deserts receive less than 10 inches (25 cm) of rain per year, but the amount that falls in a given spot varies greatly by season and by year. In the summer, daytime temperatures are scorching, but winters can be cold, with freezing temperatures and occasional frost.

Desert plants and animals have unique adaptations for these difficult conditions. For example, desert plants have hard and waxy stems and leaves to reduce evaporation and for protection from blowing

Four Peaks after a rare snow in the Sonoran Desert outside Phoenix, Arizona, March 2006. *(Pierre Deviche, Arizona State University)*

sand. Most have shallow roots to collect any water that may strike the ground surface. A deep taproot anchors the plant to the ground and exploits deeply buried water. Cacti and other similar plants store water in their main body cavities; their thick skins and spines protect them from animals that might see them as a water source. Although desert vegetation is sparse, the plants are distinctive and often beautiful, as can be seen in the Sonoran Desert of southern Arizona. Desert plants may be dormant during times of drought only to flower profusely after a rain.

Desert animals have many adaptations to these extreme conditions. Many are nocturnal, spending their days beneath rocks or in burrows. Spadefoot toads emerge from burrows in the summer only after rains create the puddles in which they breed. In dry years, the toads never emerge. Jackrabbits dissipate heat through their large ears, and camels store water within their humps. Kangaroo rats get all their water from the seeds they eat. Some desert beetles are adapted to collect the freshwater that condenses on their bodies as dew each morning.

Tropical Rain Forest

Luxuriant tropical rain forests are found between the Tropic of Cancer (22.5°N) and the Tropic of Capricorn (22.5°S). Temperatures are fairly constant, between 68°F (20°C) and 77°F (25°C) year round, and water is abundant, with between 80 and 600 inches (200 and 1,500 cm) of rain annually. These mild conditions support the greatest diversity of living organisms on the Earth, an estimated 50% to 80% of all species. The largest tropical rain forests are in the Amazon Basin of South America and the Congo Basin of Africa. Smaller tracts are located in Central America, Hawaii, and other tropical islands.

Plants are at the heart of rain forest biodiversity. Rain forests contain 170,000 of the world's 250,000 known plant species (68%). Each hectare (2.5 acres or 10,000 square meters) contains 350 to 450 tree species, and only one or two representatives of each tree species are found within a single hectare. By contrast, temperate rain forests have between 6 and 30 species per hectare, and three or four species account for almost all trees.

Tropical rain forest biodiversity extends to animal life. More than 50,000 insect species fly, burrow, or crawl within a single square mile (260 hectares or 2.6 square kilometers) of rain forest. One-third of all the world's bird species live in South America. Each hectare of rain forest has tens or even hundreds of vertebrate species. Madagascar, an island off the eastern coast of Africa that is smaller than the state

The Amazon Rainforest at the Tambopata Research Center on the Tambopata River in the Madre de Dios, Peru. The vertical layering of trees, with emergents sticking above the canopy, is seen. *(© Michael J. Doolittle / The Image Works)*

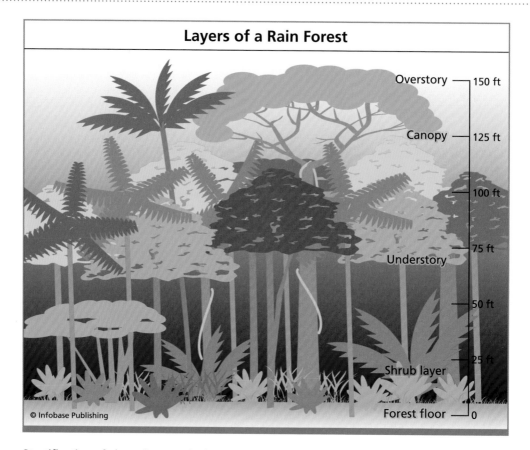

Layers of a Rain Forest

Overstory — 150 ft

Canopy — 125 ft

— 100 ft

— 75 ft

Understory

— 50 ft

— 25 ft

Shrub layer

© Infobase Publishing

Forest floor — 0

Stratification of plants in a tropical rainforest shows the emergents of the overstory poking through the rainforest canopy, which looks like a continuous green carpet from the air. Below the canopy are the understory and forest floor, where little light penetrates and so plants are somewhat scarce.

of Texas, has nearly four times as many species of frogs as the entire United States; almost all of them are endemic. An enormous number of species live in the abundant rivers and lakes.

Like temperate rain forests, tropical rain forests are three dimensional. They can be divided into five unique layers. In the topmost layer, the trees of the **overstory** rise 20 to 100 feet (6 to 30 m) above the canopy. Since they are individual trees that are not protected by the canopy, overstory trees are exposed to wind, temperature, and moisture variations. Eagles nest at the tops of emergent trees and fly above the canopy, diving down when they spot their prey of primates, parrots, or other large mammals.

The next layer, the canopy, rises 100 to 160 feet (30 to 50 m) above the forest floor, appearing from above as an impenetrable carpet of green. Amazingly, 40% of all plant species on Earth live in the rain forest canopy. Epiphytes, such as orchids and bromeliads, obtain their nutrients from other plants, and liana vines weave forest plants together. One-quarter of all insects and a tremendous variety of birds, mammals, and reptiles live in the canopy as well. Monkeys, flying squirrels, sharp-clawed birds, and other animals fly, climb, leap, or glide between the forest's trees.

Beneath the canopy is the **understory** or shrub layer. Since little light penetrates the canopy, there are a relatively few small trees, young trees, ferns, and orchids. At forest edges, along river banks, or where land has been cleared, light penetration allows shrubs and other plants to grow thickly, creating **jungle**.

Normally, so little light penetrates to the rain forest floor that it is remarkably clear of growth. Small animals climb, hop, or run through sparse vegetation, and large animals such as rhinoceroses, chimpanzees, gorillas, elephants, bears, and leopards may even travel freely. In the soil, animals burrow, and microorganisms decompose the leaf litter and animal tissue that falls from above. Rain forest soils are not very fertile because years of rain trickling through have leached them of most of their minerals and nutrients. In rain forests, new plants obtain nutrients from dead plants decaying on the forest floor.

Tropical and Subtropical Dry Forest

Forests in tropical or subtropical zones that receive ample rain in the wet season but have a long dry season (up to eight months) are known as **dry forests**. Dry forests are less well known than rain forests, and they have less biodiversity, but they are still extremely important. One example of dry forest is Costa Rica's Area de Conservación Guanacaste, discussed in Chapter 13. Because trees lose moisture through their leaves, the trees in a dry forest are mostly deciduous and shed their leaves during the drought season. This opens the canopy so sunlight can reach the ground, allowing the growth of thick underbrush. Trees in broadleaf dry forests include teak and mountain ebony. Where groundwater is accessible, most dry forest trees may be evergreens. Monkeys, large cats, parrots, and ground-dwelling birds are common dry forest wildlife.

Ocean

Oceans cover 71% of the Earth's surface; they are not uniform, but vary greatly in temperature, pressure, salinity, and nutrient level. These characteristics determine the amount and type of life found in a particular area. For example, a particular nutrient may be the limiting factor for productivity; a **limiting factor** restricts the number of individuals of a given species that can live in a given area.

Nutrients are abundant near continents, where they run off the land, and at upwelling zones, where deep-sea waters rise to the surface. Primary productivity is often greatest in those areas. The nutrients support phytoplankton, which in turn sustain rich ecosystems of invertebrates, fish, birds, and mammals. Seaweeds and sea grasses maintain nearshore ecosystems.

The oceans have great biodiversity, especially near the shore. Coral reefs are known as "the rain forests of the sea," with an estimated one-fourth of all marine plant and animal species, totaling as many as one million species. Kelp forests are good homes for snails, abalone, urchins, and other grazers that are eaten by fish, starfish, and sea otters that in turn are hunted by sharks, sea lions, and whales.

The deep sea has no plants, but harbors a great diversity of animals. Life in the deep sea is harsh because there is no light, the weight of the water above creates extreme pressure, and food is scarce. Many deep-sea species depend on bits of organic material that fall down from the sea surface. Fish move slowly and do not lose an opportunity to capture prey. Most are monstrous looking but small, between 1 and 12 inches (2 to 30 cm); they use their food for energy rather than growth. Some capture their prey with organs that light up like lures. A few have gaping mouths with jaws that unhinge to enable them to eat larger fish. To keep prey from escaping their hungry mouths, some predators have large, backward-folding teeth.

Primary productivity at hydrothermal vent communities is by chemosynthesis. Some animals live symbiotically with the chemosynthetic bacteria. **Symbiosis** is a relationship between two species of organisms in which both benefit and neither is harmed. In one symbiotic relationship, chemosynthetic bacteria live within the tissues of giant tubeworms; the bacteria provide the worms with a constant source of food and, in return, are given shelter.

Estuary

An **estuary** is a bay where fresh river water mixes with ocean water, as in the San Francisco Bay or Chesapeake Bay. Although conditions such as salinity and temperature are variable, estuaries are extremely biologically productive. Nutrients run off the land, and if the estuary receives enough sunlight, primary productivity is high. Small organisms such as snails and worms are eaten by birds such as ducks, geese, and long-billed shorebirds. Fish and shrimp use estuaries as nurseries, where eggs hatch and young grow to maturity. Other fish, such as salmon, pass through estuaries on their way to their spawning grounds. Salt marshes and mangrove forests are diverse ecosystems that are found at the transition between land and sea. **Mangroves** are flowering trees that grow in dense forests along tropical shorelines.

Inland Water

In lakes, as in the oceans, phytoplankton and weedy plants support ecosystems of invertebrates, small fish, and larger animals, with bacteria acting as decomposers. In temperate regions, lakes freeze over in winter, allowing organisms to survive in the middle and deep waters. When the ice melts in the spring, the cold melt water sinks and the deep water is pushed up to the surface. In the autumn, the upper layer cools, becomes dense, and sinks, causing the deep water to rise.

During these overturns, sinking water takes dissolved oxygen down to the life forms that live in the deep layers, and rising water brings nutrients that have collected in the deeper layers up to the surface, which may cause a burst of primary productivity.

Streams start as snowmelt or springs in mountains, then merge as they travel down slope, until they come together to form a river. The movement of water does not allow for photosynthesis, so stream ecosystems import much of their organic matter from the surrounding land, especially nearby forests. Aquatic organisms, such as fish, flow with streams and rivers, and many birds and mammals rely on streams for water and food.

Wetlands are covered all or part of the time with fresh or salt water. Extremely biologically productive areas, these poorly drained regions are varied and complex ecosystems. **Marshes** are the most common and widespread wetlands, with soft-stemmed plants such as lily pads, cattails, reeds, and bulrushes. Marsh ecosystems are teeming with waterfowl and mammals, such as otters and muskrats. **Swamps** occur in poorly drained depressions in which hardwood trees and other woody plants thrive. Swamp vegetation, such as cypress and mangrove forests, provides great habitat for invertebrates, including freshwater shrimp, crayfish, and clams, as well as fish, waterbirds, crocodiles, and such small mammals as beaver and otters.

ECOSYSTEM SERVICES

Organisms working individually and together provide crucial services to the environment and to each other. The most obvious service is the food supplied directly or indirectly to all other living creatures by photosynthetic and chemosynthetic organisms. Organisms provide habitat for other species; for example, eelgrass is a home for fish. Bacteria break down plant and animal tissue to release nutrients that are used by plants. Insects, birds, and bats carry pollen from one flowering plant to another, allowing them to exchange genetic material and create fertile, healthy offspring. Plants keep down erosion by holding soil in place with their roots. Soils contain microbes and plant materials that cleanse the water that trickles through. Soil microbes detoxify or sequester pollutants.

Living creatures undertake important interactions with the atmosphere by cycling or "fixing" atmospheric gases. Although nitrogen is the most abundant gas in the atmosphere, it is not in a chemical form that plants can use. Bacteria and algae "fix" the nitrogen—that is, modify it chemically—so that it is in a form useful to plants. Animals need plants to convert CO_2 into oxygen, and plants need animals to convert oxygen back into CO_2; thus, each life form depends on the other.

Because CO_2 is an important **greenhouse gas**—that is, one of the atmospheric gases that trap some of the Earth's heat—plants help to regulate global climate. While greenhouse gases keep Earth's temperatures moderate, and so are extremely important to living things, excess greenhouse gases make the planet warmer and can lead to **global warming**. Plants absorb CO_2. The tremendous biomass of tropical rain forests contains enormous amounts of this gas, which keeps it out of the atmosphere and so helps to regulate global temperatures. (**Biomass** is the mass of all the living matter in a given area.)

Wetlands ecosystems provide enormous benefits to the environment. Wetlands are like a bank for water: During floods, they absorb excess water; during droughts, they release water into streams. Water in wetlands seeps into the soil to recharge groundwater supplies. Wetlands also act as nurseries for young animals, including commercially valuable species of edible fish and seafood. Many plants and animals depend on wetlands for food and habitat, and many species of migratory waterfowl nest in wetlands. As water trickles through wetlands, the rich soil filters excess sediments, nutrients, and other pollutants. The aquatic organisms that live in wetlands also degrade toxins; therefore, water exiting a wetland is purer than when it entered.

WRAP-UP

Organisms live together in ecosystems; ecosystems with similar conditions are part of the same biome. Ecosystems provide organisms with food, gas exchange, and shelter. Along with their many other services, they provide climate regulation and water management to the planet and to people. Scientists increasingly realize how important ecosystem services are. For example, as climate scientists model complex climate systems, they come to understand the importance of rain forests in regulating carbon dioxide and, in turn, the world's climate.

PART TWO

THE SIXTH EXTINCTION

Extinction in Earth History

Extinction is a natural process. About 99.9% of the species that ever lived on Earth are now extinct. The end may come very slowly, over thousands or millions of years, or very rapidly, possibly within hours. Extinctions are caused by long-term alterations of the environment, such as climate change, or by catastrophic events, such as asteroid impacts. Humans also bring about extinctions by overhunting, habitat destruction, and the introduction of nonnative species. Extinction is irreversible: Once a species is gone, it is gone for good. Novels, movies, and children's imaginations aside, dinosaurs will never again roam the Earth.

WHAT IS EXTINCTION?

The evolution of new species is crucially important to the history of life. Just as important is the extinction of life forms; only about one-tenth of one percent (0.1 percent) of all the species that have ever lived on Earth is here today. Scientists estimate that in recent Earth history, without human involvement, an average of between 1 and 10 species per million has become extinct each year. Typically, a species becomes extinct about 10 million years after it evolves, but some well-adapted species, such as sharks and cockroaches, have been around unchanged for hundreds of millions of years.

Species become extinct for two very different reasons. Some species die off when their numbers fall too low to maintain a successful breeding population. Other species become extinct when they successfully evolve into new species; although that particular species is gone, its most favorable genetic traits are represented in the new species. Even some dinosaur genes live on in their successful descendents—the birds.

Many extinctions in Earth history have taken place during mass extinctions, geologically brief periods during which 25% or more of all species are wiped out. There have been at least five major mass extinction events since life began to flourish 600 MYA. Many scientists think that the sixth is currently under way. The six mass extinctions in Earth history and their causes are outlined in the table on page 55.

There are many possible causes for mass extinctions; in some cases, more than one factor may contribute to the termination of species. Some natural causes of mass extinctions are presented below.

- ⊕ **Plate tectonics**: Continents join together and break apart in cycles lasting hundreds of millions of years. Land masses also drift nearer to or further from the equator and poles. Variations in the placement of continents affect environmental conditions including climate, the availability of coastal habitat, and the circulation of ocean currents, which may alter water temperature and weather patterns.
- ⊕ Climate change: The Earth's climate has varied over its history from much hotter to much colder than it is today. If climate changes suddenly (geologically speaking), organisms that are adapted to one climate may not be able to evolve fast

The Six Mass Extinctions

TIME (MYA)	GEOLOGIC TIME	WHAT WENT EXTINCT?	CAUSE
0	Recent	Extinction ongoing	Human activities
65	Cretaceous-Tertiary boundary	85% of all species from land and seas	Asteroid impact
248	Permian-Triassic boundary	90%–95% of all species	Asteroid impact or colossal volcanic eruptions
360	Devonian-Pennsylvanian boundary	70% of all marine groups	Meteorite impact, sea level decline, or global cooling
440	Ordovician-Silurian boundary	Nearly 100 families of marine invertebrates	Unknown
544	Precambrian-Cambrian boundary	79% of all species, including most marine microorganisms	Massive glaciations

enough to adapt to the new conditions and may be driven to extinction.

⊕ Volcanic eruptions: Most volcanic eruptions only affect weather locally, but very large eruptions may blow enough ash into the upper atmosphere to cool the planet for several years. **Flood basalts**, extremely rare and voluminous eruptions of very fluid lava, cover thousands of square miles (km) with thick flows. Individual flows can be more than 160 feet (50 m) thick with volumes exceeding 480 cubic miles (2,000 cubic km). By contrast, in 16 years, Hawaii's

Kilauea volcano erupted only 0.36 cubic miles (1.5 cubic km) of flow. Gases and particles released in the eruptions could cause global warming (CO_2 and sulfur dioxide), global cooling (sulfuric acid aerosols and dust particles), and acid rain (rain that is more acidic than natural rainwater, a phenomenon caused by sulfur and nitrogen oxides), any of which could bring about extinctions. The eruptions could also bring about changes in ocean chemistry and ocean circulation.

- Asteroid impact: Asteroids strike the Earth all the time. Some are large enough to form a crater, such as the Meteor Crater, 4,000 feet (1,200 m) wide, in northern Arizona. Meteor Crater was created between 20,000 and 50,000 years ago by an iron meteorite that was 200 feet (60 m) in diameter. Although the asteroid strike that produced Meteor

The Demise of the Dinosaurs

Dinosaurs and many other species of both terrestrial and marine animals were extinguished by an asteroid impact that brought an end to the Mesozoic Era, also known as the Age of the Dinosaurs. Scientists have pieced together the story of what happened from rock and fossil evidence and from experiments and computer models: 65 million years ago, a rock 6 miles (10 km) in diameter struck the Earth with 10 billion times the energy of the atomic bomb that destroyed Hiroshima, Japan, in 1945. Ground zero was the coast of Mexico's Yucatan Peninsula, where evidence of the crater can be seen in the limestone rock of the northern side of the peninsula and beneath the waters of the Gulf of Mexico. Dust and gas from the asteroid and the limestone it struck were blasted into the upper atmosphere and spread around the planet. Some of the dust coalesced into fireballs, which rained down onto the Earth's surface, raising the temperature of the atmosphere to that of a kitchen oven on broil. Forests burned and land animals roasted. Some scientists think that the dinosaurs were extinct within an hour of the asteroid strike.

For the creatures who survived the impact, the future was bleak. Dust and

Crater probably did not cause any extinctions, a much larger asteroid is credited with the extinctions of the dinosaurs and many other species on land and in the oceans 65 million years ago.

The largest extinction in Earth history came at the end of the Permian period, 248 million years ago, when 95% of species perished. The cause is highly controversial, and no one is certain which one or more of several plausible scenarios was responsible. There are currently three hypotheses:

⊕ An asteroid impact triggered a massive release of sulfur from the mantle, which led to the loss of significant amounts of oxygen as the oxygen joined with the sulfur to form sulfur oxides, and to acid rain production.

smoke kept the Sun's light from reaching the planet's surface. Temperatures grew brutally cold, and darkness kept plants from photosynthesizing. Sulfur gas released from the limestone mixed with water in the atmosphere to form acid rain, which dissolved phytoplankton shells. With little photosynthesis from either terrestrial or marine plants, animals starved and food webs collapsed. Carbon from the limestone combined with oxygen in the atmosphere to create CO_2. Within months, global warming brought the planet from freezing to scorching.

At the end of this period of extremes, more than two-thirds of the Earth's species were gone. Most stunning was the end of the reign of the dinosaurs, which had lasted for 165 million years. Mammals, which had been a minor group during the Late Mesozoic, evolved to fill the vacant niches. Although there is evidence that factors such as climate change had caused some dinosaur species to go extinct before this event, most scientists agree that a chance hit by an asteroid 165 million years ago was at least partly responsible for setting life on Earth on a new course.

⊕ The eruptions of the Siberian Traps flood basalts caused global cooling and then global warming. Atmospheric CO_2 levels reached 10 times their present value, thereby raising global temperatures by 20° to 50°F (10° to 30°C). The extreme heat greatly altered oceanic and terrestrial conditions. Acid rain killed plants, allowing erosion to bring dirt into the sea surface, which disrupted photosynthesis and caused the collapse of the marine food web.

⊕ The Siberian Traps eruptions did not warm the atmosphere enough to cause the mass extinction, but enough to alter ocean circulation. Ordinarily, in the Northern Hemisphere, cold water sinks into deeper ocean layers and moves toward the equator, bringing oxygen to mid- and deep-sea life. If the warmer atmosphere warmed the sea surface so that it became too warm to sink, oxygen would not enter the deep sea, and only anaerobic bacteria would be able to survive. Anaerobic bacteria release hydrogen sulfide gas, which would circulate upward through the water, enter the atmosphere, and poison both terrestrial and oceanic organisms. Only green sulfur bacteria could live in this environment. Evidence for these unusual life forms has been found in rocks from that time period.

After a mass extinction, many ecological niches stay empty for a time. Eventually, though, organisms evolve to fill them. It takes between 20 and 100 million years for an ecosystem to reach the same level of biodiversity it had before the extinctions.

HUMANS AND EXTINCTION

Many biologists think that Earth is entering its sixth major mass extinction event. This extinction is due to the destructive effects of one single species—humans. Although the rate of extinction is now ramping up precipitously, people have been triggering extinctions for at least ten thousand years.

During the Pleistocene period, wooly mammoths and saber-toothed cats were among the large mammals that dominated terrestrial ecosystems. However, rising temperatures after the Pleistocene period brought about a decline in the populations of some of these mammals, and many species went extinct. Some scientists suggest that humans are at least partially responsible for these and other relatively recently extinctions, an idea known as the **human overkill hypothesis.** The extinctions were caused because people hunted to excess, destroyed animal habitats, and introduced alien species and diseases. There is a great deal of evidence for the human overkill hypothesis:

- ⊕ The post-Pleistocene extinctions did not occur simultaneously around the world, but took place later in the Americas and Australia than in Europe. The extinctions closely follow the first appearance of humans on a continent or island. The median time of extinction after human invasion is 1,229 years.

- ⊕ Only large mammals, which are easily hunted, became extinct, rather than the assortment of creatures that perish during typical mass extinctions. Using language and relatively sophisticated tools, people could hunt effectively in groups, perhaps killing far more animals than they could use.

- ⊕ The only other plausible explanation for the post-Pleistocene extinctions is climate change. This is unlikely because climate conditions changed gradually, and the extinctions were not simultaneous. Mass extinctions did not take place at the end of the previous glacial periods.

An example of human overkill comes from North America. Before the arrival of the paleo-Indians, the prairies east of the Rocky Mountains were home to the greatest diversity of large mammals the world has ever known. Mammoths, mastodons, giant ground sloths, and buffalo lived with lions, tigers, and enormous birds of prey. Within 1,000 years of the arrival of humans in North America around 13,400 years ago, all of these grand creatures were extinct. Although this may seem extremely fast for human hunters with Stone Age tools, a computer simulation published by paleobiologist John Alroy of the University of California, Santa Barbara, in a 2001 article in *Science* models the extinction as follows: A human population of 100 that grew at 2 percent annually and broke off into bands of 50 as the population increased, with each band killing 15 to 20 large animals a year, would eliminate the large animals within 1,000 years.

A similar story follows the arrival of humans in areas all around the world. In Europe and Asia, half the species of large animals— wooly mammoths, elephants, rhinos, giant deer, hyenas, lions, panthers, bison, hippos, and bears—were eliminated between 30,000 and 15,000 years ago. The extinction of large mammals and flightless birds in Australia around 46,000 years ago was several thousand years after the first arrival of humans.

More recently, people have caused large numbers of extinctions on oceanic islands. Because many islands do not have predators, many island bird species evolve to be flightless and naïve, a word biologists use to mean that they do not have the ability to respond effectively to a human threat. When humans arrive, the birds are easy prey for people and their cats and rats. Within 500 years of the arrival of the Maori people in New Zealand in approximately A.D. 1000, the island's 12 species of giant flightless birds called moas—plus many species of frogs, lizards, and other birds—disappeared. Hawaii lost more than 50 species of birds after the arrival of the Polynesians. Scientists estimate that one-fifth of all of the bird species that were on Earth a few thousand years ago have gone extinct due to human colonization of oceanic islands.

Africa is the one location where large animals and flightless birds did not die out in the same numbers as elsewhere. Proponents of the overkill hypothesis suggest that this is because humans did not invade Africa but evolved there in conjunction with the continent's fauna. Because they evolved with humans, natural selection favored highly diverse mammals, many of which were supremely adapted to running.

Slow-moving herbivores such as the ground sloth would not have been successful in Africa.

THE CURRENT EXTINCTION CRISIS

The rate of human-caused extinctions is increasing markedly, and no longer are only large mammals and island birds at risk. The millennium ecosystem assessment by the United Nations Environment Programme (UNEP) found that the current global extinction rate is between 100 and 1,000 times higher than the average over geologic time. Entire ecosystems are being lost or altered beyond recognition, and many species are in peril. An **endangered species** is any plant or animal species whose ability to survive and reproduce has been jeopardized by human activities. A **threatened species** is one that is likely to become endangered. The extinction rate in 50 years is forecast to be more than 10 times the current rate.

A letter written in May 2005 by 11 of the nation's top conservation biologists, led by Harvard's E.O. Wilson, to the Chair (Senator Lincoln Chafee) and Ranking Member (Senator Hillary Rodham Clinton) of the United States Senate Environment and Public Works Subcommittee on Fisheries, Wildlife, and Water, describes extinction this way: "Extinction is the killing off of all individuals, forever extinguishing the life of an entire species. . . . In both its scope and its irreversibility, extinction is the most frightening, most conclusive word in our language. When a species has been declared extinct, not only have all its individuals died, but the possibility of any such individuals ever existing again has been foreclosed."

The best survey of species decline in a geographic region was compiled from large numbers of surveys that took place in England, Wales, and Scotland when more than 20,000 volunteers submitted over 15 million species records collected during the 20 to 40 years before 2000. Dr. Jeremy Thomas from the Natural Environment Research Council Centre for Ecology and Hydrology in Dorchester, United Kingdom, found that 71% of butterflies and 54% of birds had population declines over 20 years, and 28 percent of native plants had declines over 40 years. Two butterfly species (3.4%) and six plant species (0.4%) became extinct. The population decreases took place in all major ecosystems and all across Great Britain.

In the March 2007 listing by NatureServe (a nonprofit organization that uses scientific information to guide conservation action), for the United States and Canada, 196 species were listed as extinct and 683 as possibly extinct out of the more than 50,000 species in their database. Another 7,568 were listed as imperiled—4,075 of those critically. Extinct organisms that once lived in the United States include the Caribbean monk seal, the Hawaiian rail, and the bigleaf Scurfpea. Birds have been hardest hit in the United States, with 2.3% of the endemic bird species gone forever, including the once unfathomably abundant passenger pigeon. Other lost endemic species in the United States are 2.2% of amphibians, 1.2% of freshwater fishes, 1.1% of plants, and 8.6% of freshwater mussels.

At the root of the problem is human population growth, which increased from 6 million when agriculture began 10,000 years ago, to around 900 million at the beginning of the nineteenth century, and to about twice that by that century's end. At the end of the twentieth century, the population increased to around 6 billion. At the minimum, all of these people need food, access to clean water and secure shelter, and a place for their wastes. Many people expect more than these basics, requiring transportation and material goods ranging from toilet paper to computers to speedboats.

"The collective actions of humans—developing and paving over the landscape, clear-cutting forests, polluting rivers and streams, altering the atmosphere's protective ozone layer, and populating nearly every place imaginable—are bringing an end to the lives of creatures across the Earth," said science writer Virginia Morrell in *National Geographic* in 1999.

Worldwide, an estimated 30,000 species are lost per year, or about 3 per hour, most of them in the highly diverse tropical regions. The World Conservation Union (ICUN) projected in 2004 that about 1 million land organisms will disappear in half a century. In all, some 12%

of birds, 20% of reptiles, at least 32% of amphibians, as many as half of the plant species, and 25% of mammals (including lions, rhinos, tigers, and most primates) could be extinct by the end of this century. Even more dire is the prediction of Harvard University biologist E.O. Wilson, who estimates that one-half of all species on Earth will be extinct by 2100.

WRAP-UP

While extinctions, even mass extinctions, are normal for the planet, the rate and causes of the current extinctions are not. For the first time, a large number of extinctions are not the result of asteroid impacts, natural climate change, or volcanic eruptions, but are due to the activities of a single species. Ever since humans evolved the intelligence to develop language and sophisticated tools, they have overhunted, altered habitat, introduced nonnative species, or otherwise compromised the habitat of many species, resulting in their extinction or the threat of their extinction. The causes of species extinction by humans will be looked at in more detail in the following chapters.

Loss of Habitat

Biologists agree that the greatest threat to life on the Earth is the degradation and destruction of habitats. Forests, grasslands, and deserts are cleared for farms and cities. Rivers are confined and dammed; wetlands are drained. Coasts are developed as cities and resorts. The land from nearly half of the planet's ice-free areas has already been transformed for human uses; by 2032, more than 70% of the Earth's surface is projected to be altered. Much of the landscape of the developed nations has already been altered, and destruction is accelerating in developing nations, particularly in tropical rain forests. A transformed ecosystem is unlikely to be the perfect habitat for at least some of the native species, and those species are likely to experience population reductions or even extinction.

HABITAT LOSS AND FRAGMENTATION

Habitat loss is the primary threat to 85% of endangered and threatened species in the United States, and possibly to even a higher percentage globally. Modern equipment—bulldozers, chainsaws, and other tools—allows habitat to be destroyed much more rapidly than it was in the past. Biologists estimate that when 90% of a habitat is lost, approximately half of that habitat's species become extinct in that region. When habitat is destroyed, plants and small animals are lost. Larger mammals and birds may be able to move to remaining habitat, where they must compete with the original inhabitants for space and nutrition.

Dividing large ecosystems into smaller islands of habitat separated by agriculture or urban land is known as **habitat fragmentation**. Habitat is lost or fragmented due to the following:

- Conversion to urban or agricultural land: Many native species cannot live in this intensely altered landscape.
- Roads built into natural areas to facilitate agriculture, logging, mining, and urban development: Roads destroy habitat and promote erosion; runoff from roads is a source of oil and other pollutants. Roads allow people to get to areas that were previously inaccessible so that they can hunt or log, either legally or illegally.
- Water development: Streams are engineered so that they no longer flood or so the water is available for irrigation and other human uses, which alters floodplains and other aquatic habitats and reduces the amount of land left for wetlands.
- Pollution: Excess nutrients, primarily from detergents and fertilizers, can alter or destroy an ecosystem. Acid rain changes the chemistry of soil, streams, and lakes, making it less hospitable to life. Toxic chemicals from pesticides or industrial uses interfere with animals' physiology.
- Fire and fire prevention: Ecosystems that would not normally burn, such as tropical rain forests and deserts, now burn due to human alteration of the environment, which can destroy the ecosystem. In other ecosystems, fire stimulates the germination of seeds or, in some ecosystems, degrades organic matter into useful minerals; but fire prevention interrupts these processes. Fire prevention also allows

organic material to build up to unnatural quantities so that when a fire does occur it is more intense and damaging.

- ⊕ Recreational activities, such as the use of off-road vehicles, allow people access to remote areas. Wildlife and their nesting sites are disturbed, plant cover is destroyed so that soil is compacted or more easily eroded, animals are run over and killed or injured, and water and air are polluted.

Rarely do habitat fragments fully represent the original habitat. The resemblance of a fragment to the original ecosystem and the number of species living in the fragment correlates with the size of the fragment. If much of the land in an ecosystem is converted to other uses, wildlife populations dwindle to a handful of individuals living in isolated pockets of habitat, separated by farms, roads, office complexes, or parking lots.

Organisms in small areas are more susceptible to stresses, such as disease and invasive species. (**Invasive** or **alien species** are organisms that have been introduced by human activities into a location where they are not native.) Diminished plant and animal populations are more vulnerable to extinction since the gene pool within these islands may become so small that there is no longer the genetic variability needed to allow organisms to adapt if conditions change. Hardships such as a small temporary change in climate may then be able to wipe out an entire population.

With forests, small fragments have a lot of edges, which receive more sunlight and wind and are therefore drier than forest interiors. The additional sunlight increases understory growth, which may foster more intense forest fires. Invasive species, pests, and domestic animals penetrate a forest from its edges. For example, the brown-headed cowbird lives at forest edges, laying its eggs in songbird nests. Young cowbirds are larger than their nest mates and steal food from the songbird's real young so that the young songbirds do not survive. When the amount of edge increases, more songbird nests are taken over by cowbirds.

DEFORESTATION

The loss of forest due to **deforestation** is the major cause of habitat loss. In all, 80% of the world's old-growth forests are gone. The temperate forests that once stretched across North America and Europe fell decades or centuries ago. Britain had chopped down nearly all of its virgin forest by 500 years ago. The United States, once a vast frontier of seemingly limitless trees, now has less than 4% of its original forest. In area, the reduction has been from 1,625,000 square miles (4 million sq. km)—equal to the area of the seven largest states: Alaska, Texas, California, Montana, New Mexico, Arizona, and Nevada, and most of the eighth, Colorado—down to only about 60,000 square miles (150,000 sq km), equal to the size of Georgia.

Boreal forest—the largest intact terrestrial ecosystem in the world (6.5 million square miles [17 million square km])—has so far largely been spared. While Siberia's forest is being logged, and Scandinavia's has been a tree farm for decades, Canada's share of the biome accounts for 25% of the world's remaining virgin forest. In early 2006, Canada committed to preserving nearly 5 million acres (20,000 square km) of virgin boreal forest, an area nearly the size of New Jersey, as wilderness. Still, every year, timber companies chop down a region about the size of Connecticut. In 2001, the province of Ontario lost 45,000 migratory-bird nests to logging.

Deforestation of all forest types—tropical, temperate, and boreal—occurs for the following reasons:

- Fuel: Half of all downed trees are used for fuel, particularly in developing nations.
- Wood and paper products: At least half of the world's timber and nearly three-quarters of its paper are consumed by 22% of the world's population: people in the United States, Europe, and Japan. Timber is used for building, furnishings, paper products, and many other commodities. Global paper use has increased six-fold since 1961.

- Cattle ranching: Ranchers clear tropical rain forests to create cattle pastures. Some of the beef is exported to developed countries and made into inexpensive, fast-food hamburgers and frozen meat products. For every quarter-pound hamburger made from cattle grazed in cleared rain forest, about 55 square feet (5.1 sq m) of rain forest (the size of a small kitchen) is destroyed.
- Agriculture: Forests are cleared for farmland worldwide.
- Resource extraction: Mining, oil drilling, and logging destroy forest habitat, and the roads built for access to these resources open up large forest areas.
- Industrial development: Pipelines, power lines, roads, dams, and other infrastructure are built to open forests for large-scale industrial development.

Cleanup of logging debris after clear-cutting a hardwood forest on the Georgia Coastal Plain. *(David J. Moorhead / The University of Georgia / USDA Forest Service)*

Logging is often done by clear-cutting, which is the harvesting of all the trees in an area. Clear-cutting often occurs in patches, a practice that creates forest fragments. Clear-cutting exposes the soil to sunshine, which bakes it and kills the decomposers, and to the rain and wind, which erode valuable topsoil. The silt muddies streams, degrading water quality and harming fish.

In selective logging, loggers take only the most valuable trees. Selective logging is more common in tropical and subtropical forests, where species diversity is high, and only some of the trees are valuable. Hardwoods, such as mahogany, are selectively logged from tropical rain forests, for example. Selective logging may cause local extinction of the preferred species and can damage other trees when a logged tree hits or pulls down other nearby trees as it falls.

LOSS OF TROPICAL RAIN FORESTS

With the temperate forests largely logged out, developed nations are turning to tropical and subtropical forests for wood products. These forests are largely located in developing nations, which are usually unable to exploit this resource on their own. Therefore, they sell the logging rights to multinational corporations that benefit not only from the timber but from the nation's inexpensive labor. About 40% of the logs are shipped to the developed nations, which produce lumber and finished products to sell on the world market. In this way, most of the forests' riches end up in the developed nations. Even so, timber exports bring just under $1 billion annually into the Brazilian economy.

Logging in tropical rain forests may be done by clear-cutting or selective logging. In the Amazon, clear-cutting has left so many forest fragments that the area that is considered forest edge may exceed the area of forest that has been cleared. In the Brazilian Amazon, selective logging has doubled the amount of rain forest that is degraded by humans each year. Most selective logging takes place illegally on land that has been set aside for conservation or for use by indigenous people. (**Indigenous** means originating in and characteristic of a particular region or country.)

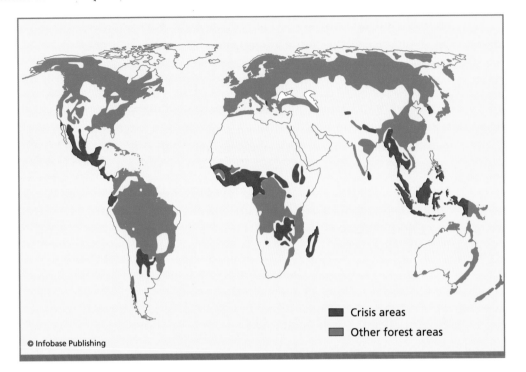

Deforestation is prevalent worldwide because developing countries and countries with growing populations need the land for homes, businesses, and roads and need the wood for building or cooking. As these forests are depleted, however, so are some of the world's most valuable and complex ecosystems.

Local people clear the rain forest by **slash-and-burn agriculture** to feed their families. The farmers slash down trees at the forest edge and then burn the unusable scrub and other material. Former rain forests make terrible farmland because of the nutrient-poor soils. After a few years, the soil is exhausted of nutrients, so the farmer grazes cattle on it. The cattle tramp down the soil, which increases erosion and leaves behind a bricklike surface layer. With the old land destroyed, the farmer clears a new plot. (Owners of large plantations have more success growing crops in former rain forest because they can afford fertilizer.) Crops grown on land that has been slashed and burned include sugarcane, bananas, pineapples, peppers, strawberries, cotton, tea, coffee, marijuana, and coca (for cocaine).

When rain forests are destroyed, the ecological services they perform are also lost. Cutting down trees keeps them from absorbing CO_2, which contributes to global warming. If the forest scrub and debris are burned (as in slash-and-burn), the plant matter releases the CO_2 it has already absorbed. Losing rain forest plants reduces the region's **evapotranspiration** (the evaporation of water by plants), interrupting the hydrologic cycle. Losing biodiversity means the loss of living species, but it also means the loss of a unique gene pool. Plants or animals with compounds that could be useful for pharmaceuticals, for example, are gone.

Tropical rain forest once covered as much as 12% of the planet's land surface (6 million square miles [15.5 million sq km]), but now only about half remains, mostly in the Amazon. About 120,000 square miles (310,000 sq km), an area nearly as large New Mexico, the fifth largest state, is lost each year, and the rate of destruction is increasing. Projections show that tropical rain forests may be gone in as little as 40 years.

THE AMAZON RAIN FOREST

The Amazon is by far the world's largest rain forest: The Amazon forest originally covered more than 2 million square miles (7 million sq km) in portions of the countries of Brazil (where 60% of the Amazon rain forest is located), Columbia, Peru, Ecuador, Bolivia, and Venezuela. What is currently taking place in the Amazon serves as an example of what is happening to rain forests globally.

The Amazon rain forest lies in the Amazon basin, the world's largest watershed, which includes the Amazon River and its 1,100 tributaries. (A **watershed** is a river, all of its tributaries, and all of the land that they drain.) Nearly one-quarter of the world's fresh water is found in the Amazon region. More than 100 inches (200 cm) of rain falls during the wet season, which lasts about 200 days. At this time, the river floods several hundred thousand square miles (km) of the countryside, although numerous small islands remain above the floodwater. Because of this variety of habitats, the

Amazon has the most biodiversity of any ecosystem in the world, with up to 30% of the world's total plant and animal species. Much of the rain forest is remote, and many of these plants and animals are still unknown.

Biologists estimate that the Amazon rain forest is home to more than 75,000 species of trees, including the rubber tree, the Brazil nut, the sapucaia, and many species of myrtle, laurel, bignonia, fig, mahogany, rosewood, palm, and acacia. In a 16-square-mile (41 sq km) area, scientists have counted 750 tree species, most with only a few individuals. Epiphytes, liana, and ferns are among the 150,000 species of other plants that thrive in the forest.

An estimated 2.5 million insect species inhabit the Amazon. Many are not very pleasant: Mosquitoes carry diseases such as yellow fever and malaria, and small biting black flies are common. Other insects include fireflies, bees, hornets, wasps, beetles, cockroaches, and cicadas. There are also hundreds of species of butterflies. Sometimes thousands of individuals can be seen gathering in a single location.

Biologists estimate that there are 15,000 species of other animals in the Brazilian Amazon. In a 16-square-mile (41 sq km) area, scientists have counted about 125 species of mammals, 400 species of birds, and 100 species of reptiles. Most of these species are endemic.

The Amazon River dolphin and thousands of species of freshwater fish live in the Amazon River, including many different species of piranhas, which, despite their bad reputation, are mostly vegetarians. The carnivorous species mostly eat other fish but will attack animals or people that enter the water. The anaconda, a snake with a length up to 30 feet (9 m), swims through shallow waters and swamps surrounding the Amazon. Endangered Amazonian manatees are the largest Amazonian aquatic mammal, at over 1,000 pounds (450 kg) and 9 feet (2.7 m) long. Crabs and turtles also live in the river habitat.

One-fifth of all the world's bird species are found in the Amazon basin. Flocks of parrots and macaws fly morning and night between their feeding and roosting grounds. Hawks and eagles soar above the forest, hunting for prey. Parakeets are more common there than sparrows are in the United States. Waterbirds include herons, cormorants, and roseate spoonbills. Toucans, endemic to this rain forest, use their large bills to eat fruit.

Among the hundreds of species of mammals is the three-toed sloth, an animal that moves only when necessary and then very slowly. The world's most primitive large mammal, the Brazilian tapir, uses its large proboscis like an elephant's trunk. The capybara, the world's largest rodent, weighs up to 170 pounds (77 kg) and lives in water and on land. Many species of bats fly about the Amazon, including the world's only blood-sucking bat species, the vampire. Jaguars, ocelots, and pumas stalk the forest searching for food. Chorusing howler monkeys join the screeching squirrel monkeys, spider monkeys, woolly monkeys, capuchin monkeys, and marmosets soaring through the trees. The forest also gives shelter to anteaters, armadillos, and iguanas.

Before Europeans entered South America, indigenous Amazonians inhabited the forest, living in small groups. They were well adapted to use the resources their environment had to offer, but they used them sustainably. (**Sustainable** resource use does not compromise the current needs for resources or the needs of future generations for present economic gain.) All groups hunted for meat using weapons such as blowguns and arrows. Forest dwellers collected fruits and nuts, while those who lived on the riverbanks fished and farmed root crops. The native Amazonians had a vast knowledge of local plants and animals: They processed the poisonous cassava (manioc) into farinha, a food that is still popular in Brazil; discovered that quinine could help combat malaria; found treatments for paralysis and other disorders; and extracted cocaine from coca leaves. The indigenous people coated arrows with poisons developed from tree bark or the skin of poison dart frogs for more effective hunting. To avoid being drenched by rain, the people waterproofed cloth with the sap of rubber trees.

As happened to many Native American groups, large numbers of Amazonians were wiped out by diseases brought by the Europeans, such as smallpox, measles, and influenza. Large numbers were taken into slavery by rubber barons. A few groups of indigenous people moved deeper into the forest, and some remain there today, although the area of remaining undisturbed forest is continually shrinking.

The Brazilian government has been actively developing the Amazon rain forest since the 1940s. The most important step was to build major roads across the forest that then became a framework for smaller roads. Roads increase economic development by allowing loggers to access and transport trees, farmers to engage in slash-and-burn agriculture, settlers to build towns, and peasants to harvest rain forest products. Rubber is an important rain forest commodity, as are some foods, such as Brazil nuts, and plants for pharmaceuticals, perfumes, and flavorings. Fossil fuels and minerals are taken from some parts of the Amazon basin, and factories and settlements are growing up along the riverbanks.

Cleared Brazilian Amazon rainforest east of Bolivia is shown in this satellite image taken on June 30, 2003. That destruction is actively taking place is indicated by the number of large and small fires burning throughout the region. Intact forest is dark green; cleared land is tan or reddish brown. *(NASA / Landsat Satellite)*

In the 1960s and 1970s, the government began subsidizing the creation of large cattle ranches, which now are responsible for more than 30% of Amazonian deforestation. About 30% of the meat is grown for foreign markets, including the fast-food industry of the United States. Although the cattle ranches are owned by the nation's political elite, the sale of beef brings in foreign capital that helps the country's economy.

The Treaty of Amazonian Cooperation, signed in 1978 by representatives of all of the basin's countries, pledges that the region will be developed based on sound ecological principles. However, despite the treaty, enormous tracts of forest are destroyed each year—currently about 10,000 square miles (25,000 sq km), an area about the size of Maryland. Researchers estimate that, at this rate, by 2020 less than 5% of the Amazon rain forest will remain in pristine condition. However, one good sign is that deforestation peaked in 1995, and Brazil is starting to better protect its forests. In the years 2005 and 2006, the amount of rain forest lost was 40% less than in 2004.

Human activities also unintentionally degrade the Amazon rain forest. Fire normally would not spread in a rain forest ecosystem because the only sparks would come from lightning, which would be accompanied by rains that would douse the fire. But now, fires from slash-and-burn agriculture escape into adjacent forest segments. The first time the fire comes through, the trees with thin bark die, but because the fire is not very hot, they do not burn completely. When the next fire reaches the area, the dead trees serve as fuel, and the destruction is greater. Dead trees also create openings in the forest canopy, allowing sunlight to reach the forest floor and increase understory growth, which also serves as fuel. Smoke from a fire decreases the forest's evapotranspiration, which decreases rainfall and makes the forest even more vulnerable to fire. With so much dry fuel, subsequent fires are much more devastating. Eventually, so many trees are lost that the region becomes scrub or grassland.

The worst drought since record keeping began about a century ago began in 2005, bringing many problems to the Amazon basin. In western Brazil, there were three times as many fires in September 2005 as during September 2004. In some areas water levels have dropped so

March 1998: Having burned through a settler's manioc field, a fire is now burning uncontrollably in the Amazon rainforest. *(© John Maier, Jr. / The Image Works)*

low that some communities that depend on streams for transportation are completely isolated. Crops rot because they cannot be transported to market, and children cannot get to school. Fish die in the shallow water, forcing people to depend on government food packages. Streams do not flow enough to remove human waste, and the backup of sewage raises fears of an epidemic of cholera and other waterborne illnesses. Stagnant pools allow mosquitoes to breed, which has the potential to increase the number of cases of malaria. The Amazon drought was blamed on high ocean temperatures in the Caribbean and Atlantic basins, which are likely the result of global warming and to the alteration of the local climate by ongoing deforestation.

Researchers say that the hope for the Amazon does not lie in keeping the forest as a giant untouchable park, because many people depend on the ecosystem for their livelihoods. Hope for the future, they say, lies in learning to use the forest sustainably. Nevertheless, development should be limited to the regions that are already developed, and people should be kept from moving farther into the forest.

WETLANDS

For nearly two centuries, people in the United States have plowed or paved over the nation's swamps and marshes. Rich wetland soils make highly productive farmlands, and sites near large rivers or the coast are desirable locations for development. These mysterious ecosystems are also home to creatures many people think of as undesirable, such as crocodiles and mosquitoes, which provides another reason to eliminate them. California has lost over 90% of its wetlands. Now, nearly two-thirds of the state's native fish are extinct, endangered, threatened, or in decline. Forested riparian wetlands near the Mississippi River once had the capacity to store about 60 days of river discharge but now can store only about 12 days. Researchers say that the flooding of the Gulf of Mexico coast from Hurricane Katrina in 2005 would have been much less extensive had the region not lost so much of its wetlands in the past century. Without wetlands, pollutants make their way more readily to streams, lakes, and the oceans. Wetlands loss is not unique to the United States; half of the planet's wetlands have been drained in the past century.

WRAP-UP

Many of the planet's resources are contained in ecosystems; some, like good soils, petroleum, or valuable metals, may lie beneath the ecosystem. Wetlands, deserts, chaparral, and most other ecosystems are being lost to allow people to gain access to these resources. Hardest hit are forests, which contain trees that are used for timber, paper, and many other products. Forests may sit above oil or mineral resources. The land beneath forests may be desirable for farms, ranches, or urban areas. When a forest is lost or fragmented, many native species of plants and animals are lost with it. Wetlands, which include swamps and marshes, also are endangered and in need of protection.

Pollution

Pollutants are the waste products of human society. They are dumped into the air or water, or onto the land. Once they are released, pollutants may travel around the globe. No location, no matter how remote, is free from modern pollutants. Some pollutants are harmful to organisms. They may inhibit photosynthesis or respiration, cause reproductive or other physiological problems, or kill organisms outright. Pollutants do damage singly, but they may do even more damage when found together or when they affect organisms that are experiencing other environmental stresses.

AIR POLLUTION

Human activities such as burning gasoline in cars create **air pollution**, the contamination of the atmosphere by gases and other substances. The Environmental Protection Agency (EPA) recognizes six major air pollutants: particulates; carbon monoxide; sulfur dioxide;

nitrogen dioxide; lead; and ozone, which is a pollutant in the lower atmosphere. Most air pollution comes from the burning of fossil fuels such as oil, gas, and coal. Burning forests and other plant materials, as in slash-and-burn agriculture, also produces pollutants. Air pollutants have a variety of ill effects, from raising global temperature, to destroying natural atmospheric processes, to causing damage to the environment and human health.

Particulates—solid particles that are light enough to stay suspended in the air—include windblown dust, saltwater droplets, volcanic ash, and particles from burned fossil fuels and plants. Particulate haze reduces the amount of sunlight received by plants and sometimes obstructs photosynthesis. Particulates provide nuclei on which water vapor condenses to form clouds, raindrops, and snowflakes. Changes in particulates in the atmosphere may change a region's temperature and precipitation. Any of these changes can alter the environment enough to be damaging to some species.

Ground-level ozone is a pollutant that comes from mixing fossil-fuel exhaust with sunlight. Ozone enters plants through their leaves, commonly slowing their growth. Forests are vulnerable to ozone pollution because trees live a long time, and ozone effects accumulate over many years. Weakened trees are more susceptible to other problems such as invasions by insects. Some trees are more sensitive to ozone than others, and if a forest's native trees become sick or die, they may be replaced by more ozone-tolerant species. With different trees forming the forest's framework, entire ecosystems can be altered. Tree species that are sensitive to ozone include quaking aspen, red maple, Jeffrey pine, paper birch, white pine, American sycamore, and flowering dogwood.

Carbon monoxide is a problem where car exhaust builds up, as in tunnels. In humans, the gas reduces oxygen delivery to organs and tissues and affects vision and motor skills. In high doses, the gas is poisonous. In the concentrations present in ambient air, carbon monoxide does not seem to affect wild plants and animals. This is not the case with sulfur and nitrogen oxides. Sulfur oxides inhibit growth in broadleaf and evergreen plants. Nitrogen pollutants injure native plants that have evolved under nitrogen-poor conditions and favor nonnative, nitrogen-tolerant species.

Nitrogen and sulfur oxides also combine with water in the atmosphere to form acid fog or rain, which can damage or destroy an ecosystem. Acid fog ruins the waxy coatings of leaves, harming a plant's ability to exchange water and gases with the atmosphere. Trees weakened by acid experience slower growth or injury, and are more vulnerable to stresses such as pests or drought. The leaves of leafy plants turn yellow, and damaged pine needles become reddish orange at the tips and eventually die. If acid rain or fog kills large swaths of trees, the organisms that depend on them may also die.

High acidity can entirely change a freshwater ecosystem. Some aquatic organisms, such as some plants, mosses, and black fly larvae,

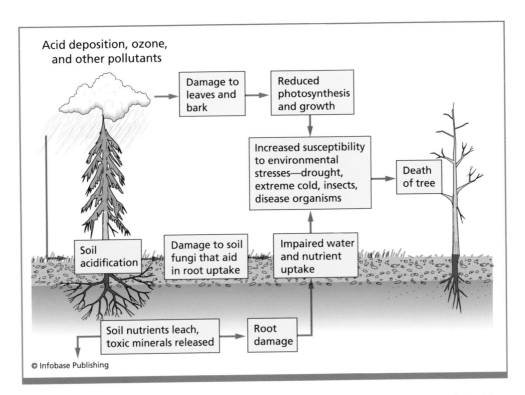

Air pollution can damage trees directly or can stress them, making them more vulnerable to other adversities such as disease, insects, and climate change.

thrive in acidic lakes and streams. But high acidity is lethal to fish and to many other plants, birds, and mammals. Frogs can tolerate higher acidity than can fish, but frogs cannot live in a lake without food. When a lake becomes so acidic that bacteria die, organic material does not decompose but stays matted on the lake and lakeshore.

Acid rain strips the soil of its nutrients and metals. Without nutrients, plant growth is reduced; trees that are deficient in calcium are less able to withstand freezing. Water carries the metals into lakes and ponds, where the metals may be toxic to fish and other animals. Acidic soil is harmful to snail populations. Without enough snails to eat, songbirds do not get enough calcium and so produce eggs with thin shells. Birds and mammals that eat calcium-deficient plants may produce young with weak or stunted bones; mammals may produce less milk.

Sulfur and nitrogen oxides can travel hundreds of miles through the atmosphere and create acid rain far from the source of the pollution. For example, the Scandinavian countries are experiencing an environmental crisis due to acid rain caused by emissions in the United Kingdom and Western Europe. Canada's acid rain problem comes largely from the United States, and the eastern United States suffers from acid-causing pollutants created in the Midwest. Rainwater in the northeastern United States has 10 times the acidity of natural rain.

The Clean Air Act of 1970 helped the United States improve the deterioration of air quality. The act established air quality standards, set emissions limits, empowered state and federal government with enforcement, and increased funding for air pollution research. As amended in 1990, the act now regulates 189 toxic air pollutants, promotes the use of alternative fuels, and also restricts the pollutants that contribute to acid rain and stratospheric ozone depletion.

Since the act's passage, emissions of the six major pollutants have dropped by 51%. A market-based system for controlling the emissions responsible for acid rain resulted in a 41% decline in sulfur dioxide (SO_2) emissions between 1980 and 2005. Nitrogen oxide emissions are thought to be less than half what they would have been without the program. This has resulted in a decrease in acid deposition in the eastern United States of as much as 36% relative to 1980 in acid-prone regions, and a decrease in the number of acidic lakes and streams of one-quarter to one-third in some areas. Emissions are reduced through the use of cleaner fuels and the installation of pollution-reducing technologies, such as cleansers on smokestacks and catalytic converters on cars. Due to the development of new technologies—hybrid vehicles, fuel cells, and clean coal, for example—the next few decades should see further reductions in emissions from power plants, industries, and motor vehicles, at least in the developed nations.

Although ground-level ozone is a pollutant, ozone in the upper atmosphere protects life on Earth from some of the Sun's high-energy ultraviolet radiation (UV). In the 1980s, scientists discovered that **chlorofluorocarbons (CFCs)** and some other manmade chemicals float into the upper atmosphere and release their chlorine ions, which then break apart the ozone molecules. Fortunately, countries are phasing out the use of these ozone-depleting chemicals by the terms of the Montreal Protocol, the international agreement that is a singularly successful global response to an environmental problem. After decades of declining stratospheric ozone levels, the rate of increase in the size of the **ozone hole**—a zone in the stratosphere above the south polar region (and, to a lesser extent, the Arctic) that has severely depleted springtime ozone levels—is declining. The size of the ozone hole is likely to begin to decrease later this decade.

The effects of ozone depletion are still being seen, however, particularly in the polar regions. Ozone loss allows UV damage to accumulate in trees; conifers and evergreens have experienced a decrease in growth rate and may subsequently change form. Tundra and subarctic plants have become stressed by the excess UV and are more vulnerable to problems such as insect infestation.

In marine ecosystems, phytoplankton appear to respond to increased UV by sinking deeper into the water. At greater depths, their contact with visible light is reduced, which causes them to photosynthesize less. When the ozone hole is overhead, Antarctic phytoplankton produce approximately 12% less food energy, possibly equaling a 2% to 4% annual loss. Scientists have calculated that a 16% depletion of ozone could result in a 5% loss of phytoplankton biomass. Lower

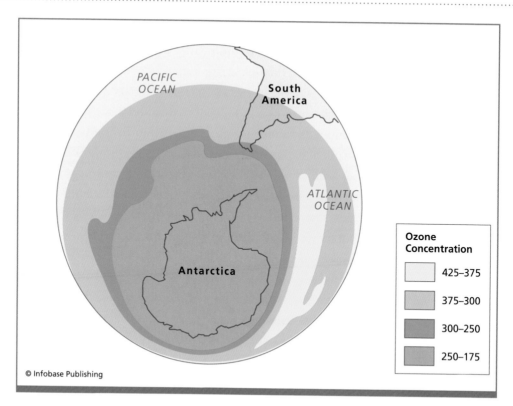

In September 2000, the ozone hole was especially large over Antarctica and the Southern Ocean, even spreading up over southern South America.

productivity at the base of the food chain means that there is less energy for reproduction and less for consumers, which could reduce populations of fish, seabirds, and several species of baleen whales.

OIL LEAKS AND SPILLS

Marine ecosystems are damaged by oil that spills from shipwrecks or other disasters. The worst oil spill in the United States was in 1989 when the *Exxon Valdez* struck submerged rocks in a narrow, iceberg-filled passage in Prince William Sound near Valdez, Alaska. The oil spread out over the sea surface, coating more than 1,100 miles (1,700 km) of shoreline.

For the first day or two after a spill, hydrocarbons evaporate off the oil, killing the larvae and young of nearby aquatic organisms. In the next days and weeks, oil floating at the sea surface reduces the sunlight available for photosynthesis, which causes primary productivity to decrease. Floating globs of oil that coat seabird feathers and mammal fur cause the animals to lose their buoyancy and insulation and perhaps drown or die of exposure. Oil globs clog fish gills and kill larvae. Chemicals released by the oil reduce spawning success in some fish; the same chemicals are linked to genetic damage and malformations in some species and reduced growth and mobility in others. Some oil sinks and smothers invertebrates that are living on or in the seafloor. The *Exxon Valdez* spill killed an estimated 250,000 seabirds, including 900 bald eagles, 2,800 sea otters, 300 harbor seals, 23 whales, and untold numbers of fish. The spill temporarily wrecked the sound's $150 million per year salmon, herring, and shrimp industry.

Plants and invertebrates that produce large numbers of young recover comparatively quickly from a spill because there are lots of opportunities for the young to find a suitable place to live. Many bird and mammal populations recover within a few years as new individuals migrate into the area once it is clean. However, in Prince William Sound, recovery of some populations of organisms may take decades. Sea otters still get oil on their fur as they try to dig up clams; their bodies contain elevated levels of toxic petroleum byproducts.

A major oil spill is a recognizable disaster, but about 10 times more oil enters the oceans each year from small leaks. These oil sources include discharge from ships, spills from oil drilling and production, illegal dumping by ships, and leaks from the outboard motors of small boats. By far, the largest source of oil in the oceans is the day-to-day **runoff** from roadways and other land surfaces. About 16 million gallons (60 million liters) of oil are carried by rivers and streams into North American coastal waters each year. The consequences of small additions of oil are less well known than those of major spills. One reason for this is that other toxic chemicals are often released at the same time as the oil. In addition, being stressed by oil exposure makes animals more vulnerable to other potentially damaging problems.

NUTRIENTS

Nutrients are essential for all living things, but in excess, nutrients are pollutants. In a natural system, nitrogen becomes a nutrient when it is fixed—modified chemically—by bacteria and algae. Now, however, humans fix nitrogen deliberately in fertilizers and inadvertently whenever they burn fossil fuels. Human activities have more than doubled the amount of nitrogen that is fixed each year. When excess nitrogen and other nutrients enter freshwater and coastal ecosystems, aquatic plants and algae flourish. When these organisms die, bacteria populations explode to consume the tissue. These bacteria use up all the water's oxygen, and without oxygen, fish and other organisms die. The depletion of oxygen in an aquatic system is known as **eutrophication**.

Because excess nutrients run off the land and enter streams, eutrophication is prominent in lakes and at the mouths of the world's large rivers. Extreme eutrophication causes animals to die or leave

© Infobase Publishing

Worldwide, there are over 140 dead zones caused by nutrient runoff. Some are constant, but others appear yearly, often during spring runoff. A percentage of dead zones appear only sporadically. Permanent dead zones often grow from episodic or seasonal dead zones.

the area, forming a **dead zone**. The dead zone in the Gulf of Mexico grows each spring and summer as the nutrient-rich waters of the Mississippi River run off the most productive farmland in North America. In some years, the dead zone is about the size of New Jersey—more than 8,000 square miles (21,000 sq km). Researchers suggest that the problem will be solved only by mandatory cutbacks in nutrient use in the Mississippi watershed; so far, only voluntary measures have been instituted.

PATHOGENS

Pathogens are disease-causing microbes (bacteria, viruses, fungi, and parasites) that infect living organisms. Pathogens may increase their range or their virulence when conditions are abnormal, such as during times of drought. Wildlife pathogens may bring about chronic diseases such as ulcers, cancer, and heart disease; botulism, for example, a disease caused by the bacterium *Clostridium botulinum*, has killed substantial numbers of waterfowl across Canada.

A pathogen can cause massive die-offs when it is newly introduced to a population that has not yet adapted to it. Hundreds of sea otters— a significant number in a population of fewer than 3,000 animals— have been found dead along the California coast each year since 2000 due to two parasites that are found in terrestrial animals. One parasite is found in opossums; the other, in wild and domestic cats. The cat parasite seems to enter the coastal ecosystem in flushable cat litters because the parasite eggs can pass through the sewage treatment system. The parasites bioaccumulate in shellfish and are then eaten in great numbers by sea otters. In **bioaccumulation**, a species that eats high in the food web collects in its body all of a harmful substance (a parasite, a pollutant) that it eats over its life cycle, and the substance becomes concentrated in its tissues. In a top carnivore, so much of the harmful substance accumulates that it may affect reproduction or cause death. Not all substances bioaccumulate; a person can take a daily dose of aspirin with no ill effect, but a daily dose of mercury will quickly build up enough to cause serious harm.

Parasites, stench, and toxic chemicals in the water system led to the passage of the Clean Water Act of 1972 (amended in 1977), which protects the streams, lakes, and ponds of the United States. The act regulates the type and quantity of pollutants that are discharged into waterways with the broader goal of restoring and maintaining the chemical, physical, and biological health of the nation's waters. In many ways, the water is much cleaner now than it was in the 1950s and 1960s. Yet pollution goals are not always met because prohibited wastes are accidentally or deliberately released into the waterways, and some pollutants are unregulated or minimally regulated.

TOXIC CHEMICALS

Chemicals used as gasoline additives, pesticides, insecticides, solvents, flame retardants, and other solutions are sometimes found to be toxic. Many of these chemicals are designed to break apart in the environment, but they often fail to do so, or the breakdown products turn out to be nearly as toxic as the original chemicals. A few chemicals are toxic in tiny amounts; for many, the effects are not yet known. Because nearly all toxicity tests are done with only one chemical, the effects of two or more chemicals acting together are also unknown. Toxic chemicals can lead to physiological and reproductive problems, such as infertility or spontaneous abortion (miscarriage), or to neurological disorders in humans or animals.

Some toxic chemicals bioaccumulate in the food web and cause problems for top predators. Dichlorodiphenyltrichloroethane (**DDT**) was commonly used after World War II for killing the insects that spread disease, including typhus and malaria. The insecticide was sprayed on plants and ponds; in waterways, the chemical was present in miniscule quantities, about 0.00005 parts per million (ppm). Algae and aquatic plants concentrated the DDT from the water to about 0.04 ppm, and small fish grazing on the algae and plants concentrated it to about 0.2 to 1.2 ppm. Top carnivores amassed DDT concentrations of 3 to 76 ppm.

Female birds were especially susceptible to the toxin because DDT interferes with their egg-laying ability. Peregrine falcons, bald eagles, barn owls, and kingfishers are just a few of the birds that laid eggs with shells so thin they would break when the mother bird sat on them. The populations of these birds plummeted, and many were placed on the endangered species list. Public outcry led DDT to be banned in the United States in 1973, and the populations of affected birds have recovered. DDT currently has very limited use in countries where malaria is rampant.

Polychlorinated biphenyls (**PCBs**) are extremely stable, water soluble compounds that once had many uses, including as flame retardants and to cool and insulate electrical devices. PCBs were known to be toxic and were never supposed to be released into the environment, but they leaked from equipment and from waste disposal sites. PCBs are extremely toxic to fish and invertebrates, even in small concentrations. The chemicals interfere with reproduction and development in birds and mammals, reducing the number and survival rates of their offspring. In mammals, PCBs interfere with the metabolism of thyroid hormones, which regulate a diversity of physiological processes, including brain development and metabolism. PCBs also reduce immune system function.

Although PCBs have been banned in industrialized nations for decades, they do not break down and are still everywhere in the environment. They are especially concentrated in top predators. Polar bears have such high concentrations of PCBs that they are losing their ability to fight common infections and are beginning to show so-called "gender-bending" effects, such as females that have male body parts. Cubs whose mothers have high PCB levels in their milk are more likely to die in their first year. Fortunately, concentrations of PCBs are dropping as the compounds become attached to sediments and are buried. In some larger freshwater lakes, PCBs in the sediments are consumed by small invertebrates, which are eaten by bottom-dwelling sport fish, making them part of the meals of fishers and their families.

Some chemicals that are still on the market behave similarly to DDT and PCBs, although not as dramatically. When more is known about these chemicals, particularly about how they act together or how they affect organisms that are stressed for other reasons, it is likely

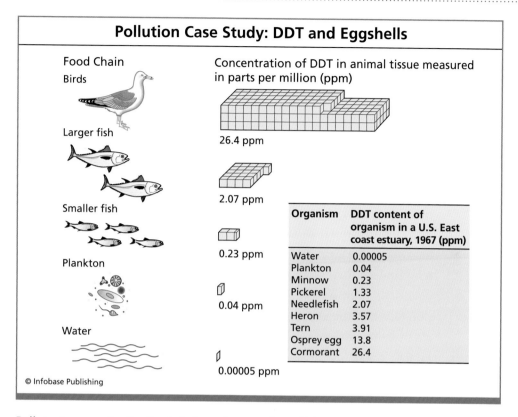

Pollution Case Study: DDT and Eggshells

Food Chain

Birds

Larger fish

Smaller fish

Plankton

Water

Concentration of DDT in animal tissue measured in parts per million (ppm)

26.4 ppm

2.07 ppm

0.23 ppm

0.04 ppm

0.00005 ppm

Organism	DDT content of organism in a U.S. East coast estuary, 1967 (ppm)
Water	0.00005
Plankton	0.04
Minnow	0.23
Pickerel	1.33
Needlefish	2.07
Heron	3.57
Tern	3.91
Osprey egg	13.8
Cormorant	26.4

© Infobase Publishing

Pollutants can enter the food chain and contaminate living organisms. In the 1960s and 1970s, populations of birds, including brown pelicans and ospreys, were badly affected by DDT, a pesticide. Here the route of contamination from polluted water to fish-eating birds is illustrated. Concentrations of DDT in this example are measured in parts per million (ppm). Because of its harmful effects on wildlife and the environment, DDT has been banned from use in the United States since 1973.

that more will be banned. Once the chemicals are in the environment, they are very difficult to remove.

The loss of birds to DDT was one factor that led to the passage of the Endangered Species Act in 1973. This act requires that the government protect all animal and plant life threatened with extinction. Species are placed on the endangered species list after intense study and public comment. The decision to include a species is supposed to be made solely on biological grounds, regardless of economic issues. Once a species is listed, the goal is for it to recover so it can be removed from the list. The act also provides recovery guidelines. For example, no one is allowed to take or harass any endangered species. In addition, the Endangered Species Act compels the conservation of the ecosystems that support threatened or endangered species.

HEAVY METALS

A **heavy metal** is literally that—a metal with high weight. Most heavy metals are found in the natural environment in low concentrations. Iron and aluminum are important components of many rocks, and mercury and lead are spewed out by volcanoes. Human activities also discharge heavy metals into the environment. Burning coal, fuel oils, fuel additives, and trash releases heavy metals into the air, as does steel and iron manufacturing. The metals eventually fall, or are rained, out of the atmosphere. Runoff from the land carries heavy metals from atmospheric fallout, mines and metal refineries, urban areas, human waste, landfills, and contaminated sediments into streams, lakes, and the oceans.

Plants and animals require tiny amounts of some heavy metals to carry out their life processes. For example, the hemoglobin molecule utilizes iron to transport oxygen in the blood. But all heavy metals are toxic to organisms in some quantity. Mercury, lead, and cadmium are not used by plants or animals and are toxic even in tiny amounts. Biologically useful heavy metals are poisonous in larger quantities.

Many heavy metals bioaccumulate. **Mercury** in organic form is especially concentrated in large, predatory fish such as tuna. The compound is easily absorbed through the skin, lungs, and guts of animals and is extremely toxic; it is poisonous to some algae and to the larvae of some small invertebrates. In humans, organic mercury causes brain, liver, and kidney damage. Recognition of the dangers of mercury to human health resulted in a great decrease in global mercury production beginning in 1990.

Tributyltin (TBT) is extremely harmful to aquatic life, in which it can cause reproductive problems. For example, exposed females of some species of freshwater snails (from the order Prosobranchia) grow penises. In mammals, including humans, TBT brings about immune-system decline. In higher doses, the compound causes neural, respiratory, and psychological disturbances, abdominal pain and vomiting, and other problems.

OTHER POLLUTANTS

Other categories of pollutants affect individual plants and animals or ecosystems. In places where the landscape has been logged, particularly on hillsides, sediment washes into streams and lakes. Muddy waters clog the gills of aquatic organisms, coat coral reefs with dirt, and keep light from entering the water so that photosynthesis is hindered. Plastic waste is ingested by marine organisms that mistake it for food; fishing nets drift through the seas, catching marine life long after the nets have been abandoned by fishers. Pollutants can also change the acidity of seawater so that shells and other structures dissolve or cannot form.

Some 70,000 different chemical substances are in regular use throughout the world, and every year an estimated 1,000 new compounds are introduced. Some of these chemicals are known to have deleterious effects in lab experiments carried out in cells or in animals. Most have not been studied, however. Of those with known effects, the damage they do may be underestimated because the harm done by a single chemical may be much less than the harm done by that chemical in a mixture. The combined effects of chemical pollutants and other environmental stresses are also unknown.

WRAP-UP

Pollution of the air, water, and land makes its way into all parts of the biosphere. Toxic substances may kill organisms immediately or may affect their reproductive success or physiology. Even beneficial substances, such as nutrients, can be harmful in excess quantities. Toxic chemicals and heavy metals may bioaccumulate, causing problems for top predators. Because the proliferation of chemicals has been happening only since the 1940s, and because more types of chemicals and greater quantities of chemicals are released each year, it is impossible to say what the long-term effects will be. Society is performing a giant chemistry experiment in which no one knows the outcome.

Climate Change

Climate change has driven evolutionary processes and caused extinctions throughout Earth history. But human activities—primarily fossil-fuel and forest burning—are now causing the Earth's climate to change at an ever-increasing rate. Warmer temperatures work together with other environmental stresses to cause extinctions. Amphibian species are being lost as global warming has allowed a certain pathogen to go out of control. As temperatures rise, many more species of amphibians and other organisms are expected to decline. Some scientists say that global warming will be the death knell for as many as one-quarter of the land animals and plants alive today.

GLOBAL WARMING

Since the end of the Pleistocene ice ages about 10,000 years ago, global temperatures have risen 7°F (4°C). One-seventh of that increase, 1°F (0.6°C), occurred in a span of only 100 years, between 1900 and 2000. And temperatures now are rising even more quickly:

Since record-keeping began in 1880, the 13 hottest years through 2006 have occurred since 1990.

The world is starting to see heat effects. Glaciers and polar ice caps are melting. Winters are shorter, and weather is becoming less predictable: Catastrophic floods, record-breaking heat waves, and unprecedented hurricane activity are now more "normal" than they were in past decades or centuries. These transformations have been attributed to global warming, which virtually all scientists now blame on human activities. Specifically, global warming is related to the release of greenhouse gases (primarily CO_2) from fossil-fuel burning and the destruction of forests. Throughout Earth history, high atmospheric CO_2 levels have been positively correlated with high global temperatures.

HOW CLIMATE CHANGE AFFECTS ECOSYSTEMS AND ORGANISMS

Plant and animal species are adapted to particular climate conditions. For example, the saguaro cactus cannot live in the Arctic. Global warming alters a location's conditions so that they are no longer tolerable for some species. In response, the species may move toward the poles or to higher elevations until it finds conditions that resemble those for which it is adapted. Those species that cannot move or adapt to the new conditions will become extinct.

Analyses show that global warming is already causing some species to move uphill (meters per decade) and others to move toward the poles (averaging 3.8 miles [6.1 km] per decade) in search of cooler conditions. Marine species are also showing up regions that were previously too cool for them—sea anemones, for example, are now found in California's Monterey Bay.

Migrating animals are changing their ranges as the result of climate change. European blackcaps, birds that have traditionally wintered in Africa, are now migrating westward to Britain in increasing numbers. Chifchaffs no longer migrate south, but remain in the United Kingdom for the winter. European butterflies are moving into new ranges: The Apollo butterfly moved 125 miles in 20 years, and the purple emperor, which first colonized Sweden in the early 1990s, has expanded its northern population. Species are also disappearing in the southern portions of their ranges.

Migration may become more difficult for many species. Many migratory birds refuel in the Sahel region of Africa before crossing the Sahara. The expansion of the Sahara into the Sahel due to decreased rainfall and overgrazing has made the journey more difficult and is likely to result in population drops in bird species such as the white-throat. Monarch butterflies travel from their wintering grounds in the mountains of Michoacan, Mexico, over the desert that lies to the north. That desert is already 400 miles (640 km) wide and is increasing in size, thereby forcing the animals to fly farther.

Not all species are able to move in response to climate change. The habitat uphill or toward the poles may be unsuitable, for example; or surrounding land may have been developed for human uses. Dr. Camille Parmesan of the University of Texas, who studies recent range changes in butterflies, told *Audubon* magazine in 2005:

> In the past when there weren't humans around, there was a lot of shifting. Between each of the [four] Pleistocene glaciations, there was a four- to six-degree-centigrade shift; species of shrews and pikas were moving a thousand kilometers north and shifting back again; spruces and oaks were going up and down mountains. The problem is that we've taken all the habitat away. It's not possible anymore for an animal or a plant to shift gradually through the scenery and end up in some spot thousands of miles away.

Biological events that are tied to temperature or to the lengths of the seasons are now occurring at different times. Spring events have advanced so that British migratory birds arrive in their breeding grounds 2 to 3 weeks earlier than they did 30 years ago. The egg-laying dates of these birds have also advanced; each 3.6°F (2°C) rise in temperature has spurred the birds to lay their eggs two days earlier. But the life cycles of the plants and invertebrates they rely on for food have advanced even more, becoming earlier by about six days for the same temperature increase. This disconnect may at some point cause problems for the birds that will hatch well after their food sources will have peaked.

Increasing temperatures are melting glaciers and ice caps. Loss of Arctic sea ice destroys the habitat required for polar bears and northern seals. Melting ice results in sea level rises, which may cause turtles and seals to lose the beaches on which they lay their eggs or raise their pups. Sea level changes may also alter the shallow coastal areas that are home to numerous species of whales, dolphins, and manatees. Coastal communities, both biological and human, are already being inundated by water during storms, and higher sea levels will just exacerbate the problem.

Temperature changes affect the breeding success of some animal species. When temperatures are high, populations of birds such as pied flycatchers increase; but some populations decrease. The sex of some aquatic animals, such as some turtles and fish, is determined by water temperature. If warmer water leads to all-female turtle hatchlings, for example, the species will die out. The effects of temperature on some species are mixed. Emperor penguins have greater hatching success when water temperatures rise, but the penguins must go farther from shore to feed.

About one-third of forests are now affected by climate change. In New Mexico, more than 45 million piñon pines have died from an infestation of piñon bark beetles—the largest loss of trees in a single location ever recorded. The combination of drought with high temperatures appears to weaken the trees, which are unable to manufacture the sap that they ordinarily use for protection against the beetles. In previous droughts, when temperatures were not elevated, the trees were not overly affected by the beetles. Scientists who study the affect of drought and heat stress on forests say that what is happening in the Southwest may be the beginning of a more widespread loss of forest ecosystems. Bark beetles are already in Arizona's ponderosa pine forests, in Utah's spruces, and in Colorado's Douglas firs. Trees in Alaska and British Columbia are also showing signs of infestation.

GLOBAL WARMING AND PATHOGENS

Most pathogens thrive in a warm environment, so global warming is expected to increase both their power and their transmission success. A dramatic example of this relationship between pathogens and warming has been seen in the past two decades in a series of cases involving nearly an entire class of vertebrates: the amphibians.

Amphibian populations are plummeting globally. Nearly one-third (1,896) of the 5,918 known amphibian species are threatened (compared with 23% of mammal species and 12% of birds), and 43% have declining populations. As many as 165 species of amphibians have gone extinct since 1980, according to the Global Amphibian Assessment's 2006 report. Frogs in the tropical regions of the Americas are suffering enormous losses—67% of the 110 species of the Harlequin frogs of Central and South America have vanished. In this region, more species have been lost in the mid-altitude cloud forests—between 3,000 and 8,000 feet (1,000 and 2,400 m), where the frogs have their greatest diversity—than in the forests of the lowlands or highlands. Habitat destruction and pollution are undoubtedly taking an enormous toll, but amphibians are dying off even in ecologically pristine areas, such as national parks.

Global warming is one environmental stress that does not recognize national park boundaries. In the last quarter of the twentieth century, tropical temperatures increased at three times the rate of the previous 75 years. In the mid-altitude cloud forests, the temperature raised 18 times as much as the average temperature increase since the end of the ice ages. Many amphibian extinctions (78% to 83%) occurred in years that were unusually warm across the tropics. Several species, including the Jambato toad of Ecuador, were last seen in 1988, after a very hot 1987.

Global warming has not acted alone on the amphibians. Warmer temperatures have been aiding a deadly pathogen, *Batrachochytrium dendrobatidis*, a chytrid fungus. This fungus weakens the animals and destroys their skin, resulting in death. The pathogen has been seen often in frog populations, but typically, the frogs rid themselves of the fungus by basking in the sun. If they can raise their temperature above

86°F (30°C), the fungus dies. But recently, at least 100 frog species in the United States, Central and South America, Europe, New Zealand, and Australia have experienced declining populations or have gone extinct due to the chytrid fungus.

The most dramatic example of the effect of climate change and the chytrid fungus took place in Costa Rica's Monteverde Cloud Forest. This forest is typical of the many cloud forests found on Central American volcanoes. Cloud forests are usually enshrouded in mist and rain, but when the mist clears, bright sunlight strikes the region. Forest plants and animals are adapted to these conditions. Warmer temperatures appear to decrease the amount of mist sitting over the forest but increase the amount of cloud cover above the mountain. Clouds obstruct sunlight and lower daytime temperatures. In response, cloud forest birds now breed at higher altitudes, lowland birds breed in the preserve, and the populations of highland lizards have declined.

The increased cloud cover keeps frogs from getting their temperatures high enough to kill the chytrid fungus, causing the amphibians to sicken and die. The extinction of the endemic Monteverde golden toad in this way was dramatic in its suddenness. The shy animals were conspicuous for only a few weeks each April, during the breeding season. In 1987, an American ecologist, Martha Crump, observed about 1,500 golden toads, the males looking like "little jewels on the forest floor." Fascinated by the animals, she returned in 1988 for further study, but no toads were breeding. Several months of searching uncovered only 10 of the animals. In 1989, only one toad was found, and no one has seen a Monteverde golden toad in the wild since. The fungus did not just take the golden toad: A 12-square-mile (30 sq km) area of the preserve harbored 50 species of amphibians in 1987; since then, 20 species have vanished.

Other pathogens have benefited from the warming climate. Nematode parasites in the Arctic and subarctic now complete their life cycles in one year instead of two. The increased number of parasites has decreased the survival and reproductive success of musk oxen. The mountain pine beetle, which carries the pine blister rust fungus, also completes its life cycle in one year rather than two,

Monteverde Golden Toads during mating season. The last member of this species was seen in 1989. *(© fogdenphotos.com)*

which affects the pine trees in the high Rocky Mountains. As warming continues, any group of organisms may find itself faced with disease from an out-of-control pathogen. Even human health may be at risk as malaria and other subtropical diseases move into the temperate zones.

THE FUTURE

Natural selection works over many generations to help organisms adapt to changes in their environment. But global warming is now occurring so rapidly that many plants and animals may not be able to adapt before they suffer large population declines. Using all of the information available to them, scientists are now trying to understand how organisms will respond to these changes.

In a report published in *Nature* in 2004, conservation biologist Chris Thomas of the University of Leeds, United Kingdom, and his colleagues used computer models to predict the number of species extinctions that global warming will cause by 2050. Thomas modeled 1,103 species—including plants, mammals, reptiles, amphibians, butterflies, and a variety of other invertebrates—that reside in six biologically rich regions that collectively represent 20% of the Earth's land surface. Each species was assumed to be able to tolerate only the set of climatic conditions in which it lives today.

The computer models projected the species responses to three possible temperature increases: minimum (1.4° to 3.1°F [0.8° to 1.7°C]), mid-range (3.2° to 3.6°F [1.8° to 2.0°C]), and maximum (above 3.6°F [2.0°C]). The following extinction rates were calculated: 18% for minimum, 24% for mid-range, and 35% for maximum. The losses predicted by the mid-range model exceed those expected from habitat destruction during that same period. According to Dr. Thomas in a 2004 University of Leeds press release, "If the projections can be extrapolated globally, and to other groups of land animals and plants, our analyses suggest that well over a million species could be threatened with extinction as a result of climate change."

As dire as these predictions seem, they may be somewhat optimistic. The models looked solely at temperature effects, although other climatic changes, such as mist in cloud forests, may hinder species survival. Moreover, Thomas and his colleagues looked only at species extinctions by 2050; other species will certainly be lost after that. Additionally, climate change is occurring in tandem with other environmental changes, such as invasive species and habitat loss.

To prevent as many species extinctions as possible, the environment will have to be well understood and heavily managed. For example, land can be kept open for a cold-loving species to migrate up a mountain. For land to be available for migrations, habitat loss and degradation should be reduced or eliminated. Unfortunately, this action seems unlikely. Furthermore, there are many cases in which a species, such as one that already lives on top of a mountain, can go no farther.

Reducing the over-exploitation of species will also help keep organisms from going extinct. Large populations of a species have enough individuals to migrate into an area that has experienced population decline. Large populations are also more likely to have the genetic diversity needed to adapt quickly to climate variations.

The best way to reduce species loss from climate change is to halt or severely limit human activities that lead to increases in atmospheric greenhouse gases. Switching to more energy-efficient technologies, developing energy sources that do not emit greenhouse gases, and learning to remove CO_2 from the atmosphere are all part of the solution.

WRAP-UP

Climate change is having an enormous detrimental effect on amphibian populations worldwide. These sensitive animals have been called the "canary in the coal mine"—the organism that dies first when environmental circumstances deteriorate. The response of amphibians to environmental changes should serve as a warning that other organisms may also be in peril. As Andrew Blaustein and Andy Dobson concluded in *Nature* in January 2006, "The frogs are sending an alarm call to all concerned about the future of biodiversity and the need to protect the greatest of all open-access resources—the atmosphere."

Over-harvesting Animals and Plants

More than one-third of the world's endangered birds and mammals are threatened directly by human activities such as fishing, hunting, and trading. Fish are harvested unsustainably as greater demand brings more boats and more modern technology to each fishery. In the past, hunting caused the decline of many species in developed countries; in developing nations, hunting now threatens many species that are harvested for meat and other commodities. Wild animals are also captured as pets or for skins and other luxury items. Plants are taken for gardens or as ingredients in herbal medicines. About one-quarter of the wildlife trade is in endangered plants and animals. Regulating this illegal trade is virtually impossible, as large profits encourage risk taking and corruption.

OVERFISHING

For millennia, the oceans supplied fish and seafood to people without fish populations being noticeably affected. Fishers cast lines from the shore or small boats to harvest fish for their families and their communities. With their reproductive strategy of producing large numbers of young, harvested fish were easily replaced. But the advent of industrialized fishing, exploding human populations, and the rising expectation that seafood should be widely available have rapidly increased the demand on fisheries.

To meet this demand, many of the world's fisheries are being overfished. **Overfishing** occurs when more animals are taken than are being replaced by young. Overfishing is the result of modern fishing techniques, which catch more fish and are more destructive to the fishery than traditional methods, and an increase in the number of boats that are harvesting from each fishery. In its 2006 biennial report, The State of World Fisheries and Aquaculture (SOFIA) and the United Nations Food and Agricultural Organization (FAO) estimated that two-thirds of fish stocks on the high seas are overfished, while most stocks close to shore are failing or are being fished to the maximum. In all, 25% of stocks are overexploited, and 52% are fully exploited. In the United States, the Office of Fisheries Conservation and Management says 41% of species in United States ocean waters are overfished.

The situation for individual species is no better. Seven of the top 10 marine fish species are fully or overexploited; harvesting increases would have serious consequences to their populations. Populations of large fish have been so decimated that only 10% of tuna, marlin, swordfish, sharks, cod, and halibut remain relative to their numbers in the 1950s. A *Science* magazine report in November 2006 projected that populations of all species of wild seafood will collapse before 2050 if fishing practices are not drastically altered. Yet, according to the United States National Marine Fisheries Service, global seafood demands will more than triple from 2004 to 2025.

The North Atlantic cod fishery on the Georges Bank off the United States and Canada provides a distressing example of fishery collapse. For 400 years, fishers harvested cod with handlines or longlines from small boats, with no detrimental effect on the fishery. When huge factory trawling ships joined the hunt in the late 1950s, productivity increased. It peaked in 1968. Subsequently, despite increased effort, fish catches dropped. By 2000, the population of mature fish was estimated at 97% below 1990 levels, which already were very low. No one knows whether the current fishing moratorium will bring the cod back because the bottom trawlers used by the industrial fishing boats destroyed the seafloor habitat that the young fish need to survive. When a fishery collapses, fishers move to new fisheries, perhaps in deeper waters or in tropical or polar waters farther away from the nations that practice industrialized fishing. But these fisheries themselves soon become overfished.

Fishery collapse has repercussions for the rest of the ecosystem. The decline in the Alaska pollock population—from an estimated 12.2 million tons in 1988 to 6.5 million tons in the early 2000s—may have led to a 94% decrease in Steller's sea lion populations in some regions. When the anchovy fishery off Peru collapsed, the famous "Bird Islands of Peru" lost about 75% of their seabirds. In Kenya, overfishing trigger fish in coral reefs has allowed the population of sea urchins to explode and damage the reefs.

To combat overfishing, fisheries must be better managed. Many marine experts favor the expansion of **marine reserves**, or "no take" zones. Marine reserves are natural systems that sustain greater biodiversity than protected areas where fishing is allowed. Marine managers can study marine reserves to more successfully supervise sites outside the reserves. Marine reserves provide a bank in which species remain unharmed so that individuals may be moved to other exploited areas, if the need arises. Less than one one-hundredth of one percent (0.01%) of United States waters are currently closed to all fishing. New Zealand and Australia (primarily within the Great Barrier Reef Marine Park) have national networks of marine reserves.

Freshwater fisheries are also being overfished, although in the developed nations, intense management is helping some fisheries to recover. Other fish, such as the lake sturgeon of the Great Lakes, remain critically endangered. Little management takes place in the fisheries of many developing nations. For example, many large freshwater fish in the Mekong River of Southeast Asia, including the world's largest freshwater fish (the Mekong giant catfish), are endangered.

Consumers can play a role in reducing overfishing by buying fish and seafood wisely. Information on whether fish and seafood is being harvested sustainably can be found online in lists kept by the Blue Ocean Institute (Guide to Ocean Friendly Seafood), Environmental Defense (Oceans Alive), and the Monterey Bay Aquarium (Seafood Watch Program).

HUNTING

Early humans hunted animals for food, warm clothing, and other commodities. As agriculture developed, farmed foods provided a larger portion of people's diets. Hunting became a sport, often reserved for the privileged classes. Many large animals have been felled by big-game hunting, also called trophy hunting. Favorite targets have included moose, caribou, bear, and elk in North America; reindeer, elk, and wolf in Europe; tiger, leopard, elephant, and wild goat in Asia; and antelope, gazelle, zebra, leopard, lion, giraffe, rhinoceros, and elephant in Africa. Small-game hunting targets small birds, rabbit, woodchuck, raccoon, and squirrel. Innumerable species have been hunted to extinction or nearly so: buffalo, the passenger pigeon, and top predators such as the cheetah.

Colonial America provides many examples of animals that once were unfathomably numerous but were hunted into extinction or near extinction. When Europeans arrived, the American bison, also called the buffalo, covered the Great Plains of the United States and Canada, with a population estimated at about 30 million animals. Daniel Boone, the American frontiersman, said of the animals in his book, *The Adventures of Colonel Daniel Boone*, first published in 1784, "The buffalo were more frequent than I have seen cattle in the settlements, browsing on the leaves of the cane, or cropping the herbage on those extensive plains, fearless, because ignorant, of the violence of man."

The enormous animals provided plentiful meat for settlers in wagon trains as they moved west. When locomotives shortened the trip, and the meat was no longer needed, railroad companies paid hunters to destroy the herds so that the animals did not interfere with the progress of trains by standing on the tracks or sheltering in the cuts dug into mountains. Buffalo were so unwary that a hunter could kill as many as one hundred in a single outing; one hunter claimed to have killed 20,000 over his career. Hunting bison had another purpose: The Plains tribes of Native Americans who were often at war with the United States depended on them for sustenance; without the bison, politicians reasoned, tribes would be much easier to control. As buffalo populations dwindled, suggestions that the animals should be protected were ignored. By 1890, there were fewer than 750 bison left, all in zoos or protected areas. From these few have come the 350,000 modern bison, most of which are not pure, but are fertile hybrids with domestic cattle.

Passenger pigeons did not fare even as well as the buffalo; they were hunted to the last bird. Scientists estimate that the animals were the most abundant bird species on Earth, approximately 5 billion birds, before the arrival of the Europeans. The pigeons lived in enormous flocks; the largest flock, of 2 billion birds, darkened the sky for several days as it flew overhead. Up to 100 nests were built in a single tree. Because they lived so close together and were slow flyers, passenger pigeons were extremely easy to hunt. Pigeon meat was so cheap, it was fed to hogs and slaves; the meat also became popular in large cities. Although everyone could see that the population was declining, no one thought that the birds were at risk for extinction because no one anticipated that as their numbers fell, the pigeons would stop breeding. Scientists now think that the pigeons' mating instinct was triggered by the presence of a great flock. As the flocks were decimated, so was the birds' desire to reproduce. The last remaining flock, approximately 250,000 birds, was killed by sport hunters in a single day in 1896. The very last passenger pigeon died in captivity in 1914.

Species of marine mammals—primarily whales, dolphins, seals, sea lions, sea otters, and manatees—have also been hunted to extinction or near extinction. For centuries, these animals were exploited for their fur, oil, and meat. By the late nineteenth century, the Guadalupe

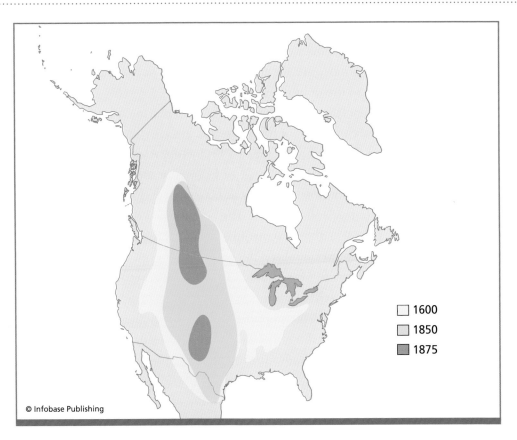

Buffalo once were a thriving species, roaming vast stretches of North America in the millions. Native Americans and European settlers hunted the animals for food, commercial purposes, and sport, however; and the population dwindled to about 300 in 1893. Congress passed a law in 1894 to protect the species, and it has since grown to about 250,000.

fur seal, found only on Guadalupe Island off of Baja California, Mexico, was down to seven animals; from those seven, the population has grown to about 1,500 animals. At the same time, the last eight known northern elephant seals were collected by the Smithsonian Institution; but a previously unknown population of about 400 animals was later discovered, and elephant seals are now abundant. (Of course, because all members of both species are descended from a small number of animals, they have a low amount of genetic diversity, which may make them more susceptible to diseases or other adversities that may arise.) Dolphins were accidentally lost in great numbers in tuna-fishing operations, but the advent of dolphin-safe fishing techniques has increased the dolphins' population.

Those success stories do not apply to all marine mammals. Despite protections, two-thirds of these species globally are now classified as threatened. The Marine Mammals Protection Act of 1972 bans taking (harvesting, hunting, capturing, or killing, or attempting to do so) or importing any marine mammals or mammal products in United States territorial waters and fisheries. The act also makes it unlawful for any person or vessel subject to the jurisdiction of the United States to harvest any marine mammals on the high seas, except under a preexisting international treaty. Many other countries have similar laws, but whaling and sealing still continue in some areas. Besides hunting, other environmental stresses, including terrestrial pathogens, are keeping some species of marine mammals from recovering.

Hunting land animals in developed nations is now highly regulated. These laws, in conjunction with wildlife refuges, have been designed to save significant populations of game animals and birds. When hunting is allowed, it is strictly regulated: The time and length of the hunting season and the sex of the allowed animals are chosen so that species do not suffer population declines.

Hunting is sometimes used as a wildlife management tool. In the absence of predators, populations of deer and other prey species sometimes exceed the ability of the habitat to support them, and in unchecked numbers they threaten the health of the ecosystem or human safety. Hunters reduce the number of animals so that the survivors have enough food and shelter to lead healthy lives. For example, limits have been removed for hunting some species of geese, which have become so numerous that they are destroying the Arctic and subarctic breeding grounds of many species. Professional hunters are sometimes hired to control animals in populated areas, such as bears in parks. Modern American hunters support conservation efforts to protect their sport by buying land to set aside or by lobbying governments for game-animal protection.

Hunting opponents say that the benefits of hunting are overrated: The sport is cruel, most hunted species do not need population control, and shooting with a high-powered rifle and other modern technology is not sport. The difference between a human hunter and a predator is that the predator chooses prey that is easiest to kill—animals that are old and sick—but the recreational hunter goes for animals that make the best trophies or that are the most thrilling to hunt. These animals are likely the healthiest, and removing them from the breeding population is detrimental to the species. Some predators are still hunted, despite the fact that they have already suffered large population losses. The hunt is extremely regulated, however.

Some native people retain hunting rights in the developed nations. The Inuit of the Arctic trap and hunt animals for clothing and footwear and make waterproof kayaks from sea-mammal skins. The Marine Mammals Protection Act contains provisions for native people to hunt seals and whales, provided the species are not endangered.

Hunting in many countries, though, is not well regulated. Over-hunting is the major problem for one-third of the birds and mammals threatened with extinction; hunting is the major threat to 8% of critically endangered mammals. As hunting technology improves, large mammals continue to be targeted except where they are specially protected. The hunting of animals, many of them critically endangered, for their meat—also known as bushmeat—in developing countries is discussed in more detail in the following section.

WILDLIFE TRADE

The sale and exchange of wild animals and plants and the products made from them is known as the wildlife trade. Plants are gathered from the wild and sold for gardens or herbal medicines; animals are sold as pets, or for food, exotic leather products, furs, musical instruments, and medicines. The wildlife trade is overseen by the Convention on International Trade in Endangered Species of Wild Fauna and Flora (CITES). CITES is administered by the United Nations and has been signed by more than 160 countries, including the United States.

The treaty prohibits international trade in threatened or endangered organisms, which now include more than 28,000 species of plants and 5,000 species of animals. In March 2007, the vertebrates on the list totaled 125 amphibians, 735 reptiles, 1,692 birds, and 919 mammals. Critically endangered species such as tigers and Asian elephants cannot be traded by member countries at all. Less imperiled species, such as many parrots and corals, can be traded only if member countries prove that the trade is being done sustainably.

According to TRAFFIC, a wildlife trade monitoring network whose task it is to monitor CITES, the international wildlife trade is currently worth as much as $12 billion and involves some 500 million animals and plants annually. Only drug trafficking accounts for the exchange of more money on the international black market. Most international trade is in species that are legally traded; each year, the United States receives about $1.5 billion in legal wildlife imports. About one-quarter of the animals and plants are threatened or endangered and are smuggled over borders illegally. Many protected animal or plant species end up as food, as pets, or in Chinese medicine shops. Because CITES only regulates international trade, no one knows how extensive or damaging the wildlife trade is within countries.

Bushmeat

Bushmeat is commercially hunted wild animal meat, often from Africa. For many generations, African forest people hunted wildlife, but forests were immense, and access was extremely limited, so the hunted animals were easily replaced by young or migrants into the area. Several factors have now come together to completely change the nature of wildlife hunting in the African forests. The forests are being heavily logged (by European and Asian companies), and hunters are using logging roads to penetrate much deeper into the forest and to gain access to protected preserves. As forest is lost, animals are forced into smaller spaces, often within these same preserves, making them easier to hunt. The hunters are no longer working to feed their families or villages, but are selling the meat to logging camps and oil and industrial towns within Africa.

As Charlie Furniss wrote in *Geographical* magazine in January 2005, "Not only do the loggers provide access for hunters . . . but they indirectly support the trade by supplying wire for snares and allowing their vehicles to transport shotguns and ammunition to the forests and meat to the markets; some even hire hunters to provide meat for their workers."

Because Africans from forested regions prefer the taste of bushmeat to domesticated meats, bushmeat is available anywhere African immigrants live, including New York, London, Paris, and other large cities. Officials estimate that up to 10 tons (9,000 kg) of African bushmeat arrives in London each day.

Recent studies show that between one and five million tons of wild animal meat are taken annually from the Congo Basin in West Africa—six times the amount that is considered sustainable. Three-quarters, by weight, is from hoofed animals such as antelope, but the rest is from predators and other large or scarce animals, including 22 species of primates. Of the mammals, 60% are harvested unsustainably. Many of these animals are among the six species of great apes.

What to do about the bushmeat trade is controversial. Scientists at the Zoological Society of London favor controlling the trade so that the meat is harvested sustainably. They say hunting is necessary because the meat is an important source of protein and cash for some of the poorest people in the world. They would impose a hunting moratorium only on critically endangered animals.

"The bushmeat trade can be very emotive and some of the pictures that come out of the bushmeat markets can be quite horrifying to western eyes but the important thing to remember is that people who are hunting and eating bushmeat generally do not have any other options,"

Central Africa: Monkeys killed by subsistence hunters are displayed by the roadside for sale to passing motorists. *(Martin Harvey / Peter Arnold)*

The Great Apes

Of the seven great ape species, only humans are not facing extinction; experts think it is possible that most species will be extinct within a generation. Chimpanzees have dropped from approximately 2 million in the 1960s to 200,000 today. The poorly known bonobo numbered between 30,000 and 100,000 in the mid-1990s and is now down to between 10,000 and 50,000. Western lowland gorillas have decreased by 50% over the past 20 years with less than 100,000 remaining. Critically endangered mountain gorillas are down to a few hundred animals, although protection has allowed populations to rise slightly from around 620 in 1989 to 700 today. Between 1900 and 2003, populations of Sumatran orangutans dropped 93%, to 7,000, and Bornean orangutans dropped 76%, to 55,000.

The reasons for the decline of great apes are familiar: habitat loss, pathogens, and the rise in the bushmeat trade. Deforestation is the biggest threat to orangutans, as the Southeast Asian forests are felled to make room for palm oil plantations. In Africa, loggers hunt the apes for meat and then sell their babies as pets. Because of their close relationship to humans, disease is a tremendous problem for the great apes. As apes increasingly come into contact with people, they are exposed to diseases for which they have no immunity, such as flu and pneumonia. Ebola, which causes uncontrollable bleeding in humans and apes, kills nearly 100% of its victims. The disease is currently rampaging through gorilla territories in the Republic of Congo and is spreading throughout equatorial Africa.

All species of great apes are protected from hunting and trade by international and national laws, but many of the developing nations in which great apes reside do not have the money to enforce these laws. Ape conservation has been especially difficult in the 11 African nations that have experienced recent civil wars. War refugees have no choice but to use bushmeat as a source of food and rangers are helpless to enforce laws in war zones.

The Great Apes Survival Project (GRASP) of the United Nations is charged with reducing the threat of imminent extinction faced by the great apes. In December 2005, the governments of 27 nations; scientists; and environmental, business, and community groups signed the Kinshasa Declaration, thereby pledging to "do everything in our power to ensure the long term future for all great-ape species and to encourage the citizens of the world, in whatever capacity, to assist and support" a global great-ape conservation strategy. Only time (of which little remains) will tell whether this effort will be effective.

said Dr. Guy Cowlishaw to BBC News Online in September 2003. "It would be a crisis if the bushmeat resource disappeared. We have a duty to make sure it remains for local people and is sustainable for the future of the species affected by it."

Other scientists do not agree. Dr. Jane Goodall, who has been a world expert on chimpanzees for decades, says that the meat is not being used to feed starving people but is being sold to people outside the community who have access to other protein sources. Hunters, she says, burn the forest to smoke out the animals and then shoot them with automatic weapons as they flee. As Dr. Goodall told the BBC in June 2002, "The animals have gone, the forest is silent, and when the logging camps finally move, what is left for the indigenous people? Nothing."

Other factors besides the destruction of important animal species come into play. Besides humans infecting apes with deadly diseases, as described on page 112, African apes and monkeys harbor pathogens that can jump into human populations. The introduction of HIV, the virus that causes AIDS, into humans has been traced to the consumption of chimpanzee meat. Jumps like these are made more likely when contact between apes and humans increase.

To stop the wholesale destruction of African animals, Heather Eves of the Bushmeat Crisis Task Force based in Washington, D.C., calls for a variety of different approaches. Governments should allow the sale of bushmeat, but only to local people. Eaves denies that bushmeat can be harvested sustainably if it is sold more widely. Eves told *Science News* in February 2005, "There is no evidence of sustainable trade where bushmeat is transported for long distances, not when biodiversity itself is being conserved." So far, though, when enforcement is tried, the bushmeat market just goes underground.

Africa is not the only continent being raided for wild animal meat. As China's economy grows, so does its demand for exotic foods such as pangolin, a slow-moving anteater. China's forests were once full of pangolins, but now they are so rare in China that illegal wildlife traders import them from distant tropical forests in Sumatra and elsewhere. Even there, the animals being captured are getting smaller, and pangolin meat is now extremely expensive: about $100 for

2.2 pounds (1 kg). The pig-nosed turtle is now hunted in remote locations in Indonesia, and reef fish are imported to China from islands off the coast of Africa. Eventually, those who strive to protect wildlife predict that the shipments to China will dry up, but not before more animals go extinct or become critically endangered. To stop this from happening, animal welfare groups are beginning to appeal to Chinese consumers. They are aided by the fear of pathogens spreading from wildlife to humans. For example, wild civet cats, a popular Chinese food source, are probably responsible for the spread of the SARS virus

Five Reasons Not to Acquire an Exotic Pet

People own exotic pets because they live in smaller spaces, have less time for attention-seeking pets like dogs, and because exotic pets are fashionable, rare, and expensive. Whether these pets are bred in captivity or captured in the wild, the Humane Society of the United States uniformly opposes keeping wild animals as pets for the following reasons:

⊕ Appropriate care for wild animals requires special facilities, expertise, and lifelong dedication. Most wild animals bond to only one person and cannot be cared for by anyone else; that person can never go on vacation. Wild cats, no matter what their size, can be deadly. Many exotic animals live a long time: monkeys up to 30 years, apes around 60 years, and parrots up to 80 years.

⊕ Baby animals grow up. An adorable baby animal that depends on its caregivers will quickly grow into a big and strong adult that depends on instinct, possibly resulting in destructive or dangerous behavior. Monkeys and apes can be up to seven times stronger than humans and as adults will revert to their instinctive behaviors of biting and scratching. Occasionally, a large cat will kill someone. Not uncommonly, an overwhelmed owner will confine a wild animal to a small cage, where the pet is later found, malnourished and cramped. Unwanted pets may be set free, possibly becoming part of the invasive species into humans. (SARS killed 774 people during the winter of 2002–2003.) Disease outbreaks from the wildlife trade are thought to have caused hundreds of billions of dollars of economic damage globally.

Exotic Pet Trade

Exotic pets are animals that have not been domesticated and often do not live well with humans, and yet the trade thrives, especially in the United States, the European Union, and Japan. More animals have become available in the past two decades as roads have been built

problem. Sanctuaries can take some unwanted wild animals, but there are not enough spots for all of them.

⊕ Wild animals spread disease to domestic animals and humans. Each year, reptiles infect 90,000 Americans with salmonella, a bacterial infection that causes abdominal pain and diarrhea. The herpes B virus is common in macaque monkeys and can be fatal to humans. In 2002, an outbreak of monkeypox in humans was traced to pet prairie dogs that had been infected with the virus by Gambian giant pouched rats from Africa that were kept in the same facility.

⊕ Whether they were taken from the wild or bred in captivity, nondomesticated animals are not adapted for life in confined conditions. Domesticated animals were bred over thousands of years to depend on humans for food, shelter, and affection. Wild animals are driven by their instincts to be self sufficient and do not need or desire human interaction.

Capturing wild animals threatens their survival. Millions of animals—60% to 70% of some birds and reptiles and 80% to 90% of reef fish—suffer and die on their way to the pet shop. Because reptiles are ectothermic and roam widely in their native habitats, they do not adjust well to artificial conditions, and untold numbers die shortly after they reach their new homes. Animals taken are often harvested unsustainably; some of them are even threatened or endangered species.

A captive juvenile black-faced spider monkey (*Ateles paniscus*) with a leash around its neck. *(Joel Sartore / National Geographic)*

deep into forests and international transportation has become ubiquitous and relatively inexpensive. Among the animals available for purchase are baboons, chimpanzees, rhesus monkeys, tigers, lions, ocelots, wolves, black bears, three-toed sloths, wallabies, foxes, raccoons, skunks, snakes, tarantulas, scorpions, turtles, lizards, birds, and coral reef fish.

Harvesting wildlife for pets damages animal populations and the ecosystems they come from. A good example is coral reef fish, which are harvested for the aquarium trade or for food. New types of gear have made fishing easier, and some modern fishing practices damage or destroy the reefs themselves. Divers squirt sodium cyanide solution at fish to stun them, making them easier to collect. If these fish are sold to the aquarium trade, they will likely die within a few months from effects of the poisoning. The sodium cyanide also kills the coral, which destroys the reef and its ecosystem. Outboard motors allow fishers to harvest animals from reefs that were once remote, and improved transportation has expanded the distance fish can be transported. As a result, the market has expanded, and demand has increased.

Reptiles and birds dominate the exotic pet trade. Birds are highly regulated by the U.S. Wild Bird Conservation Act of 1992, which bans the importation of wild birds except under narrow circumstances. The legislation reduced parrot imports to the United States from more than 100,000 birds to only hundreds annually and has resulted in a sharp decline in poaching. Most birds legally sold in the United States are captive-bred or are nonthreatened finches. Unfortunately, much of the rest of the world still allows wild birds to be traded; of the 50 threatened parrot species that are still traded, 32 species are traded legally. Popular species have suffered from the pet trade: the Spix's macaw from Brazil is now believed extinct in the wild, and many species (hyacinth macaw, blue-and-yellow macaw, and red-crowned parrot, for example) are considered at great risk.

By contrast, the majority of reptiles sold for pets are wild caught. Low transportation costs and large profit margins have made the reptile trade a lucrative and expanding business. According to TRAFFIC, millions of reptiles are traded globally each year, and about 2 million live reptiles and 6 million reptile products make their way into the United States. Increasingly, reptiles destined to become pets are being bred in captivity because they are of better quality, are used to being in captivity, and are less likely to have parasites and other health problems. Green iguanas, which account for about one-third of the reptiles imported into the United States, are raised on ranches and farmed. North American red-eared slider turtles account for most American reptile exports. Unfortunately, captive breeding is more expensive than taking reptiles from the wild, so it is likely that the trade in wild-caught reptiles will continue indefinitely.

Mammals are also part of the exotic pet trade. Although domesticated mammals are wonderful pets—dogs have deservedly earned the name "man's best friend"—wild mammals are often terrible pets. Despite this, people collect tigers, lions, monkeys, and many other exotic species.

While CITES binds each of its signatory countries to protect threatened or endangered organisms, every country also has its own laws in place to protect wildlife. The Lacey Act requires that the United States uphold the laws of these countries and of each of its states. The Exotic Pets Law of 2003 controls the exotic pet trade, making selling or owning big cats as pets illegal. Because there is so much money to be made, people in the wildlife trade often find ways around these protections. In some parts of Africa, for example, if a species is protected in one country, traders simply truck it into a neighboring country where it is not protected so that it is not in violation of the Lacey Act and can be shipped legally into the United States.

Exotic wildlife coming into the United States is monitored by the United States Fish and Wildlife Service. Although this is an enormous task, fewer than 100 inspectors are spread over 32 points of entry. Most are stationed in the most important ports: Miami, Los Angeles, and New York. Mike Osborn is an inspector in Los Angeles. As he told *The Scientist* in 2004, "We see millions of fish and thousands of reptiles. Sometimes I stop and think, 'How long can this last? How long can the world's wildlife withstand this volume?'"

When inspectors seize banned organisms at these ports of entry, they must do something with them. The coral reef exhibits in most major aquariums display confiscated exotic corals. Other animals might be donated to zoos, nature centers, schools, and universities, but there are usually many more organisms than can be used.

Increasingly, animals are being farmed for the pet trade, providing a sustainable income for local people. For example, a butterfly farm at the edge of a Costa Rican forest supplies tropical butterflies to preserves in the United States and elsewhere.

Medicinal Plants

About 80% of the world's people still use traditional medicine, including medicinal plants, to treat illnesses. China and India are two of the world's largest markets for medicinal plants. In developed countries, growing interest in alternative medicine expanded the use of medicinal plants about fifteen-fold between 1990 and 2000. Alternative medicines are a $3 billion a year market in the United States. Europe imports one-quarter of the world's herbal medicines.

Most medicinal plants are gathered from the wild and are an important income source for people in some cultures. Yet expanding populations and more widespread use has made the exploitation of some medicinal plants unsustainable. Although collecting and trading threatened plant species is regulated in some nations, many other countries, particularly in Africa and Latin America, do not regulate plant collection, or the laws are inadequately enforced. With only a small chance of being caught and a large amount of money to be made, traders have little incentive to quit plant collection. Wild Asian ginseng, for example, sells for tens of thousands of dollars per kilogram, which results in a large amount of this plant being smuggled out of

Russia each year. American ginseng is well regulated, but poaching still takes place.

To protect wild medicinal plants, regulations to see that they are harvested sustainably must be enacted and enforced. Cultivation of medicinal herbs should become more widespread, as is happening in Europe. Consumers can help to protect wild plants by asking suppliers to provide only sustainably collected or cultivated herbs.

Traditional Chinese Medicine

For more than 3,000 years, the Chinese have been using natural ingredients from plants, animals, and minerals to cure everything from the common cold to fevers, arthritis, and sexual dysfunction. These medications are sold throughout China and other Asian countries and to Asians around the world. Additionally, alternative medicine practitioners in western countries are using ancient Chinese medicines more frequently. Expansions in the market due to population increases and more widespread use, coupled with reduced habitat, have caused some important medicinal species to become endangered or threatened.

Traditional Chinese medicines use ingredients from hundreds of species of plants and animals. Many are widely available including chicken gizzard, aloe vera, and mulberry. Other ingredients come from species that are endangered, threatened, or protected. Since 1970, more than 90% of wild rhinoceros have been slaughtered for their horns, which are used to treat fever, convulsions, and delirium. Saiga antelope horn is used for cooling blood and quenching toxins, tiger bones as a pain killer and an anti-inflammatory, musk from musk deer as a stimulant for circulation, green bile from bear gallbladders for eye and liver ailments, and ginseng roots as a health tonic. Other protected animal species whose parts are used to make traditional medicines include sea lions, macaques, pangolins, crocodiles, green sea turtles, freshwater turtles, tortoises, water monitor lizards, cobras, ratsnakes, and giant clams.

Thousands of medicinal items are imported into the United States each year and about 30% of them contain ingredients taken from endangered or protected species. Many medications are smuggled

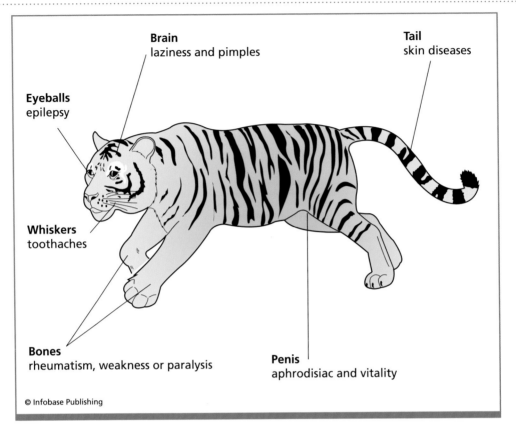

Brain
laziness and pimples

Tail
skin diseases

Eyeballs
epilepsy

Whiskers
toothaches

Bones
rheumatism, weakness or paralysis

Penis
aphrodisiac and vitality

© Infobase Publishing

The tiger is highly valued in Chinese traditional medicine. Various cures are ascribed to a number of tiger body parts.

into the country because they are not approved for sale by the United States Food and Drug Administration (FDA). The Rhino and Tiger Product Labeling Act makes it illegal to sell, import, or export (or attempt to do so) any product for human consumption or application that contains—or even claims to contain—rhino or tiger parts. The United States also regulates or prohibits trade in other traditional medicine ingredients of conservation concern, including rhino horn, musk, bear gallbladders, and American ginseng.

National laws and international treaties to halt trade in endangered or threatened animals have limited effectiveness. Huge profits, widespread corruption, weak financial backing of enforcement agencies, and a lack of political interest create a situation in which laws are easily disregarded. Enforcement officers are sometimes bribed to ignore infractions. To keep the inspectors from finding them, illegally traded animals are packed in boxes that are hidden in or behind containers that carry legal animals.

Although contraband seizures have increased lately, this is largely due to growth in the wildlife trade, not to more effective government control. Indeed, less than one percent of natural-resource crimes are punished. Even when violators are caught, they pay their penalty and return to the illegal activity. For example, Philippine fishers using dynamite and cyanide on reefs make an average of $70 per trip but pay only a nine-cent fine if caught.

WRAP-UP

Overharvesting wildlife reduces plant and animal populations around the world. The problem will continue until world attention turns to the illegal wildlife trade, and governments create and enforce laws to stop it. Consumers have the power to slow the illegal wildlife trade by asking questions before purchasing a wild plant or animal or a wild-originating product and only buying those that are harvested sustainably or are cultivated. Governments must take drastic action to save the most threatened species, such as the great apes, which are being harmed and killed by habitat destruction, overharvesting, and disease.

Invasive Species

Invasive species are organisms that enter into an ecosystem where they are not native, usually as the result of human activities. The number of alien species found around the world is growing exponentially as remote places become more accessible and shipping becomes ubiquitous. Many aliens blend into their new habitat and actually increase biodiversity with their presence. A few wreak havoc on the local ecosystem and the man-made infrastructure. Monitoring, controlling, and even eradicating invasive species is a major and extremely costly business for state and federal governments.

INTRODUCTION OF AN ALIEN SPECIES

Species naturally enter new environments frequently (after all, that is how speciation occurs), but the number of species introductions and the rate at which they are introduced has increased dramatically as people and goods move freely around the world. Human transport essentially eliminates the world's natural barriers, enabling species to interact that would have never have come into contact otherwise.

Some invasive species are moved for good reason: Most North American agricultural plants and animals are native to Europe, South America, or elsewhere. Others are brought for folly. The pesky European starling was introduced to North America in the late nineteenth century by "The American Acclimatization Society," which had the goal of establishing every species of bird mentioned in William Shakespeare's works in the United States. (In *Henry IV*, Hotspur proclaims, "Nay, I'll have a starling shall be taught to speak nothing but 'Mortimer'. . . .") Invasive species are transported unintentionally in boats, in suitcases, and on the soles of shoes.

When members of an alien species are introduced into a new ecosystem, there are three possible outcomes. In most cases, the habitat is inhospitable, and the invader perishes. Alternatively, the invader finds the habitat to be acceptable and develops a modest population, increasing the ecosystem's biodiversity. Rarely, the alien species outcompetes the native species for food and living space. If the alien has no predators, its population explodes, and the native species' population may be wiped out. If more than one native species is eliminated, the ecosystem experiences a decrease in biodiversity.

Invasive species may cause harm to native organisms other than those with which it competes. This may happen in three ways:

- ⊕ Predation: In its 50 years on Guam, the Australian brown tree snake has eliminated 9 of 13 native bird species by eating them.
- ⊕ Spreading disease: Birds introduced to Hawaii thrive in part because they are far less susceptible to the resident avian malaria parasite, also an introduced species, than are native birds.
- ⊕ Altering the environment: The Australian melaleuca tree is spreading through the Everglades; oil in the tree's leaves burns easily, spreading fires that kill native plants.

Habitat degradation and invasive species are two problems that are often linked. Habitat disturbance makes an ecosystem less livable for native species; the habitat is more vulnerable to invasion, and invaders alter natural systems. Whole ecosystems may become completely altered, as has happened in South Florida and Hawaii.

INVASIONS OF AQUATIC ECOSYSTEMS

Alien species have damaged both marine and freshwater ecosystems. The main path for an alien species into an aquatic ecosystem is the ballast water of a ship. Ships suck water—along with any organisms or their larvae swimming or floating in it—into tanks as counterbalance to heavy loads. As many as 300 species of organisms have been found in the ballast water of a single ship. When the ship dumps the ballast water, these organisms are expelled with it.

The biggest alien species disaster in the United States so far arrived in ballast water from the Caspian Sea. The zebra mussel, a small mollusk, has had enormous impacts on the Great Lakes system. The organism is a voracious filter feeder and reproducer; a single female spews out between 40,000 and 1 million eggs per season. Since they were first discovered, about two decades ago, the mollusks have spread to 20 states; in some locations, there are as many as 70,000 individuals per square foot (929 square cm). Zebra mussels drive out native species and clog drain pipes. Together, the United States and Canada spend about $140 million a year on zebra mussel damage and control.

Aquarium dumping is another common path for the invasion of an aquatic system by alien species. When their aquariums become problematic, aquarium owners dump the inhabitants into the nearest stream, lake, or pond, where they may become alien species. For example, milfoil was a lovely aquarium plant that was released into the eastern United States in the 1940s and arrived in the waters of Washington State in 1965 and British Columbia in the 1970s. It spreads from lake to lake as fragments are transported on boat trailers. Milfoil forms very dense mats at the surface of a lake, interfering with recreational activities and power generation. The mats prevent wind from mixing oxygen from the atmosphere into the lake water, which starves fish of needed oxygen. The plants also shade native aquatic plants, so they cannot photosynthesize, which causes a decline in species diversity. Milfoil is eaten by some native bird species but is not as good a food as native plants.

Ocean ecosystems are also vulnerable to alien invasions. Scientists know of about 50 nonnative species off New England's coast; more than 250 invasives are thought to live in the San Francisco Bay. One recent arrival, the sea squirt, is causing problems off the New England coast and the west coast of North America. Several species of sea squirt from the genus *Didemnum* were discovered in 2002 in small dense mats more than 100 miles (260 square km) off New England. One year later, sea squirts blanketed more than 6 square miles (16 square km); in 2006, patches of squirts covered more than 88 square miles (230 square km). The animals are now found from Connecticut to Maine and off California and Washington. Nothing seems to eat them, and they can reproduce either sexually or asexually; even a tiny fragment of a sea squirt can replicate into a new colony. The squirts coat the seafloor, smothering everything in their paths, including shellfish beds. A seabed coated with *Didemnum* is inhospitable to fish eggs. The animals also spread over aquaculture facilities and man-made structures, such as docks and piers.

The National Aquatic Invasive Species Act of 2005 was introduced to provide money for research, to monitor and control new and existing threats, and to regulate ballast water. The act followed earlier acts that responded to the zebra mussel invasion. Actions taken as a result of the 2005 act will cost $836 million over several years, a small amount compared to the $122 billion invasive species are estimated to cost each year.

INVASIONS OF TERRESTRIAL ECOSYSTEMS

Terrestrial ecosystems are also suffering from invasive species. Even the Galapagos Islands, revered for their importance in biology as the place that inspired Charles Darwin to develop the theory of evolution, have nearly as many introduced species as natives. The Hawaiian Islands are known as the islands of extinction, due in part to the enormous impact invasive species have had there.

Island animals are susceptible to invasives because the species are naïve. For example, without predators, some bird species lose the ability to fly. With the arrival of humans, many of these flightless species go "the way of the dodo." The dodo is a classic example of the damage that invasive species can do. This large, flightless bird lived on the island of Mauritius in the Indian Ocean, where it had no predators to fear. When the Dutch arrived, 400 years ago, they thought the bird foul-tasting and did not eat it, but their dogs and pigs and the rats that had sneaked on board their ships greatly enjoyed the easy-to-obtain dodo eggs. In less than 100 years, the Dodo was extinct.

Native bird species on the island of Guam have been devastated by Australian brown tree snakes, which are up to 12 feet (3.7 m) long. The snakes arrived sometime after World War II and for decades were barely noticed. But with a favorable environment and no predators, Guam turned out to be the snakes' island paradise. There are now more brown tree snakes (up to 13,000) per square mile (2.6 square km) on Guam than any type of snake on any square mile in the world. The snakes have essentially eliminated 9 of the 13 native bird species; even Guam's national bird, the flightless Koko, survives only in a compound behind an electric fence. Brown tree snakes have a venomous bite, which they use on about 200 people a year. The snakes are everywhere on the island, including inside the transformers on power poles, resulting in electrical problems that cost about $1 million a year.

Continental areas are also vulnerable to invasive species. Alien species do so well in Florida with its subtropical climate and abundant wildlife, that experts estimate that about 3,500 alien species have established a foothold there. This includes about 1,200 species of plants, which amounts to between 27% and 31% of all Florida's vegetation. Because of competition from invasives and habitat loss, more than 25% (14,000 square miles [36,000 square km]) of the state's nearly 54,000 square miles (140,000 square km) has been drained of

One night's capture of Australian brown tree snakes in Guam. These snakes are responsible for the extinction or near extinction of 9 of the island's 13 endemic bird species. *(Photo courtesy of U.S. Geological Survey)*

water. Florida has 112 endangered and threatened species: 55 plants and 57 animals, including the West Indian manatee, finback whale, gray wolf, six species of sea turtles, and many species of small mammals. Bird biodiversity in Florida has declined by 30% in the past two decades.

South Florida is the most invaded region in the contiguous United States. Vegetation in some areas has been almost entirely replaced by Brazilian pepper and melaleuca, resulting in a dense forest canopy that keeps native plants from growing and that provides a poor habitat for native wildlife species. Grasses introduced in the 1940s to feed cattle have replaced natural prairie and marsh. Weevils from Mexico are eating their way through the native bromeliads. Farmed tilapia and catfish are transported to new freshwater bodies, driving out native bass, perch, bluegill, and snook. Nile monitor lizards are slowly colonizing the entire state, having been released into the wild by people who bought the cute babies as pets but could not handle the 6- foot-long (1.8 m) adults. Giant pythons are hindering attempts to restore the natural ecosystems in the Everglades, where one python was seen swallowing an alligator whole (both animals died).

INVASIVE SPECIES CONTROL

Wildlife managers can attempt to control invasive species before they enter a new environment, early on in an invasion, or after they have become a serious problem. The action the managers take depends on how well established the invader is in its new environment, how much damage it is doing to the ecosystem, and how high the economic costs are of its being in that habitat.

The most effective way to keep down alien species damage in a location is to stop the aliens from entering; but with so many paths invaders can take, this is difficult and costly to do. Massachusetts has begun using volunteers to search the state's beaches, docks, and other locations for its 20 most wanted marine invaders. When a potentially dangerous species is identified, a strike team is mobilized to eradicate it. The state has also banned the buying and selling of over 140 plant species.

Hawaiian wildlife has suffered enormous losses, including the extinction of 23 endemic bird species, due to human hunters, disease, rats, and the mongoose. The state currently has 317 species on the endangered species list, most of them endemic—about 30% of its plants and 40% of its birds. The task of protecting Hawaii's remaining native species is enormous. Wildlife managers inspect people entering the islands for any plants, seeds, insects, and other unwelcome organisms they may consciously or unwittingly be importing. People's bags are sniffed for contraband by specially trained beagles.

A tremendous effort is being made to keep the Australian brown tree snake from establishing a hold in the Hawaiian Islands. Several of these snakes have been found at airports, perhaps having arrived in the wheel wells of airplanes. The snakes were destroyed, but no one knows if other snakes may have escaped into the forest, where they may be quietly multiplying. Because females can lay 150 eggs in a lifetime and can lay them even several years after mating, only one single adult female could start an ecological invasion.

Once they enter a new habitat, most alien species blend into the ecosystem. If wildlife managers determine that the species should be eliminated or controlled, the methods used will depend on the type of organism and how well established it is. Alien species with limited ranges—either small islands or small, isolated ecosystems—are relatively easy to control. In more difficult cases, attacking the problem in the wrong way may just make it worse. For example, introducing a new alien species as a predator may result in an ecosystem with two problem species. Or a lot of money may be spent with little or no improvement in the situation.

Mechanical methods of stopping invasive species work for invasions that have not gone too far or in areas that are limited in size. Weedy plants can be pulled if there are not too many—an approach that has been successful with the Restharrow in California. Trees can be chopped down with chainsaws, and herbicides can be used to stop seedlings.

Some animals may be stopped by trapping or hunting. Nutria—a large, South American rodent—feeds on the root mats of marsh vegetation. Without its roots, the mat becomes unstable, the mud beneath it erodes, and the marsh is replaced by stagnant pools of water. Nutria have now colonized the Gulf of Mexico region and moved up the Atlantic seaboard. After nutria in the Blackwater Wildlife Refuge in Maryland destroyed 6 square miles (16 sq km) of marsh and damaged about half of the rest, hunters were hired to eradicate the animal over a two-year period. Although the refuge has now been declared nutria free, some biologists think that some of the wily animals must have escaped death, and their populations will inevitably grow. If the program was successful, the $2 million cost was well spent because marshes protect coastal regions from storm surge and flooding.

Chemical controls on invasive species include poisons such as herbicides and insecticides. A species of Mediterranean seaweed was eliminated from two lagoons in California in 2000 by the use of chlorine. A poison that kills sea lamprey larvae ended the decimation of native fish populations in the Great Lakes that occurred between the 1920s and the mid 1950s. More recently, the chemical pheromones the lampreys use to attract mates have been used by wildlife managers to round up adults. Research into using pheromones to attract the brown tree snakes of Guam and induce them into traps is ongoing.

Biological control, or **biocontrol**, uses introduced organisms—a pathogen or a predator—to control invasive species. Biocontrol does not eliminate the targeted alien but reduces its population density. However, many past attempts at biocontrol turned out to be disastrous. In 1883, for example, sugar plantation owners in Hawaii became tired of the rat infestation (rats were an invasive species) and ordered a shipment of mongooses from the West Indies to control them. Unfortunately, because rats are awake at night and mongooses are awake during the day, the mongooses did not hunt the rats but instead went for the native ground-dwelling birds, such as the nene.

Despite this history, Hawaii now has a biocontrol program. Maui's worst invasive plants are from Brazil, so Hawaiian scientists have gone to the tropical nation to search for insects, fungi, or other pathogens that will attack them. When possible, biocontrol species are identified, and tested for effectiveness in Brazil and then shipped to quarantine labs on Hawaii, where they undergo years of tests to be sure that they will not harm native organisms or commercial crops. Several biocontrol species are now being prepared for release into the wild.

Invaders are left alone if there is no real way to eliminate them. Although efforts are being made to keep *Didemnum* from spreading to new locations, no one can figure out how to remove the sea squirt mats from the seafloor. Plant species such as the Brazilian pepper in South Florida are also virtually impossible to eliminate without doing enormous damage to the rest of the ecosystem.

In 2003, the World Conservation Union (IUCN) estimated the annual global cost of invasive species at more than $400 billion. Damages and control costs related to all invading species in the United States are estimated at $137 billion per year, according to a study by

Cornell University ecologist David Pimentel, which was published in *Science* in 2000. Florida alone spends about $260 million.

There are perhaps two ways to look at invasive species. No one doubts that the arrival of the Australian brown tree snake in Guam has been a disaster for that island's ecosystem; but Alan Burdick, who writes extensively on invasive species, argues that most invasive species do not do much harm; instead, they blend in, making the ecosystem in some ways richer than it was. As Burdick told *Discover Magazine* in May 2005, "Invasions don't cause ecosystems to collapse. That's what Florida illustrates so vividly. If anything, there's more nature running around there than ever before. . . . But unlike, say, the clear-cutting of a forest or the poisoning of a lake, invasions don't make ecosystems shrink or disappear."

However, Harvard University's famed ecologist E.O. Wilson sees the situation differently. Wilson says that in removing natural barriers to species movements, the nature of wild places is changing. Unique animal and plant communities are being replaced with a generic, impoverished hodgepodge world of hardy generalists: a world not of Sumatran rhinos, golden turtles, Blackburnian warblers, and giant saguaros but merely one of cats, rats, crows, and West Nile virus.

WRAP-UP

After habitat destruction, invasive species are thought to be the second greatest cause of biodiversity loss. Invasive species enter all types of ecosystems. Most are benign, but a few cause significant damage to ecosystems and to property. The Australian brown tree snake has devastated the ecosystem of the island of Guam, and the zebra mussel has caused billions of dollars of damage in the Great Lakes system. The best way to avoid destruction by alien species is to stop the organisms from entering the new environment. Once they are integrated into the ecosystem, most invaders are very difficult or impossible to remove.

PART THREE

SAVING BIODIVERSITY

Why Biodiversity Is Important

Without the services provided by organisms and the ecosystems they live in, the planet could not support life. People benefit from the same ecosystem services that other organisms do and use their intelligence to exploit the biosphere in ways other organisms cannot, such as for clothing, housing, and fuel. Humans rely on biodiversity to improve their lives; for example, for the discovery and use of the medications they use to combat and treat disease. Humans are also the only species that seeks to understand and appreciate the natural environment. These interests attract tourists into regions where the populations may have limited sources of income. For these and many other reasons, the preservation of biodiversity appears to be in the best interests of modern society.

BIODIVERSITY PRODUCTS

In the developing world, many populations rely on wildlife for at least some of their food, shelter, and energy. The loss of these organisms can be a serious problem for people who are already impoverished. The developed nations rely on the oceans and lakes for some protein, but most food and cloth in developed lands comes from domesticated animals and plants. Some people argue that only domesticated organisms are needed now, and biodiversity is no longer important. They say that modern domesticated animals and plants have undergone artificial selection for good breeding ability, high productivity, and other traits that have made them highly successful, and that these organisms are all people need to survive.

For many reasons, survival requires more than a planet populated by domesticated species. As a by-product of the creation of domesticated species, artificial selection has greatly reduced the genetic diversity of these plants and animals. This loss of alleles reduces the ability of a species to adapt to changed circumstances, which means that when breeders need to improve a crop or animal—perhaps to survive drought, to live in more saline soil, or to weather warmer temperatures—they must turn to wild populations for genes. If biodiversity is lost, the chance that useful genes will be available when needed is reduced.

If conditions change a great deal, such as during a continued rise in temperature, some domesticated species may no longer be successful, and replacement species will be needed. Agriculturalists will need to look to wild plants and animals to develop crops that can live in these altered conditions. At this time, the natural world offers a great many possibilities: The number of plants that could be harvested for food is estimated at approximately 75,000, but only 150 of them have ever been cultivated on a large scale. Currently, only 20 plants produce 90% of the world's food. Maintaining biodiversity assures that useful crops will be able to be developed in the future.

Beyond food and fiber, some very unusual products come from wildlife. For example, thermophilic bacteria that were discovered in hot springs at Yellowstone National Park contain an enzyme that is now used for DNA fingerprinting in forensics and diagnostics. Horseshoe crabs have a protein in their blood that is used to detect bacteria in medical implants and in injectable medicines and vaccines. No one knows how many more compounds are out there in the wild, waiting for someone to discover their usefulness.

HUMAN HEALTH

Biodiversity is important for human health for two reasons: to reduce the spread of some diseases and to supply compounds for pharmaceuticals. The incidence in humans of Lyme disease—a nonfatal bacterial infection that causes fever, headache, and joint swelling—is lower where there is much vertebrate biodiversity. Because Lyme bacteria are spread by ticks, the more species of animals the ticks can bite that are not good vectors for the disease, the more dead ends the Lyme bacteria will meet. Also, if vertebrate species are available to compete with such Lyme bacteria hosts as the white-footed mouse in the eastern United States, host populations will be kept low, which lessens disease risk.

Biodiversity is extremely important for the development of pharmaceuticals. To enhance their chance of survival, some organisms manufacture chemicals that make them attractive to mates or deter predators or competitors. A few of these compounds become the active ingredients in medicines that help to cure or slow the development of human diseases. More than 75% of the top 150 prescription drugs are derived from, or are synthesized to mimic, chemicals found in plants, fungi, bacteria, and vertebrates.

About 25% of pharmaceuticals are from rain forest organisms; their worth is an estimated $20 billion annually. Rain forest compounds include the basic ingredients of birth control hormones, stimulants, and tranquilizers. The rosy periwinkle, found in the tropical forests of Madagascar, is used for an effective children's leukemia drug. At this time, the United States National Cancer Institute has identified over 2,000 tropical rain forest plants with the potential to fight cancer.

Other ecosystems that house species that have been used for pharmaceuticals are deep sea sediments, where several antibiotic drugs, including streptomycin, have been discovered. Temperate forests contain the Pacific yew tree, the source of the cancer treatment drug Taxol, and foxglove, which has supplied the important heart medication digitalis. At this time, given the enormous numbers of organisms that have not even been scientifically described, scientists have a limited idea of how many animals and plants could provide compounds for future medications.

"Every time we lose a species, we lose an option for the future," said Sir Ghillean Prance, the director of Kew Gardens in *National Geographic* in 1999. "We lose a potential cure for AIDS or a virus-resistant crop. So we must somehow stop losing species, not just for the sake of our planet but for our own selfish needs and uses."

THE VALUE OF ECOSYSTEM SERVICES

Ecosystems provide the ecological services described in Chapter 3. Pollination (which is needed for many domesticated as well as wild plants), flood control, erosion control, climate regulation, and water filtration are all beneficial to society. Yet people tend to take these services for granted, assuming that living organisms and ecosystems will continue to provide them.

Traditionally, a dollar value has not been placed on ecosystem services; the ecosystem is thought to provide the service free of charge. More often, now, economists and planners are calculating the economic value of these services. A well-known example involves New York City and its drinking water. New York has long benefited from the services of the Catskill watershed, which filtered the city's excellent drinking water. But expansions of agricultural, urban, and industrial development into the watershed have caused drinking-water quality to dip below the minimum standards set by the EPA. Two Columbia University economists, Geoff Heal and Graciela Chichilnisky, have calculated the cost of the two options facing the city. The city could build a water purification/filtration plant at a cost of $6 billion to $8 billion, with annual expenses of about $300 million. Alternatively, the city could buy and restore the watershed, letting natural processes filter the water as they always have, for around $1.5 billion and few annual expenses. Predictably, the city has gone with the latter option and is buying land to protect the watershed.

PROTECTING NATURE FOR ITS OWN SAKE

Humans evolved in natural ecosystems: The sights and sounds of nature developed human senses, and the complex natural environment stimulated human intelligence. Of course, the natural world was not always pleasant; it held uncertainty and danger. For these reasons, most modern people have removed themselves from nature as much as possible.

Many people still find solace and inspiration in the natural world, however. The popularity of bird-watching, hiking, and other activities that bring people into the natural environment suggests that many people value the great outdoors. These activities often have economic value, as people travel to natural places for these experiences. Tourism brings a great amount of money into countries where it is needed. Some tourism, known as **ecotourism**, specifically attracts tourists who are interested in the experiences provided by the natural world.

Tourists generally spend their money in museums or at beach resorts, and on the travel, meals, and amusements associated with such places; but ecotourists additionally spend their money on the experience of visiting wild land, such as a forest, desert, coral reef, or other ecosystem. Ecotourism strives for minimal impacts on the environment. Local communities receive money by providing visitors with shelter, food, and guides, even in the ecotourism areas that are least developed. Ecotourism creates jobs for local people, and the influx of money helps land conservation and gives the locals the incentive to preserve the land as wilderness. Fees charged to park users may also be used for habitat preservation.

If managed well, ecotourism may also contribute to the conservation of the cultural heritage of the local people. Ecotourism operators may include local and indigenous people in the planning, development, and operation of their businesses. Many ecotourism operators support international human rights and labor agreements. While traveling, ecotourists are educated on both the natural and cultural resources of the local environment by being made aware of the political, environmental, and social climates of the local populations.

WRAP-UP

Biodiversity has enormous value for people. Healthy ecosystems supply people with food, clothing, water, medicine, shelter, and many other services. In some cases, people have put a dollar value on an ecosystem service, such as the cost of the filtration service provided by the Catskills watershed to New York City. In other cases, a calculation would be virtually impossible; for example, what is the value of the pollination of domesticated crops by insects? The natural world has an intrinsic value for people all on its own. Ecotourism not only deepens people's awareness of the natural world, but also contributes to the economic and cultural well-being of the local people.

Saving Endangered and Threatened Species

Biodiversity can be preserved by safeguarding genetic diversity, species diversity, and ecosystem diversity. The best way to save a species is to save its ecosystem (a topic discussed in Chapter 12). A species' genes can also be saved by placing live organisms in captivity, such as in a zoo or botanical garden, so that the captive organisms' genetic material is available to supplement that of wild or other captive populations.

SAVING SPECIES IN THE WILD

The best way to save a species is to preserve a genetically viable population in an ecosystem that can support it. Saving ecosystems requires preserving a habitat and enough of its organisms for the population to be genetically viable. This may require limiting or banning hunting and other forms of wildlife trade. Both international and national efforts are under way to save species in the wild.

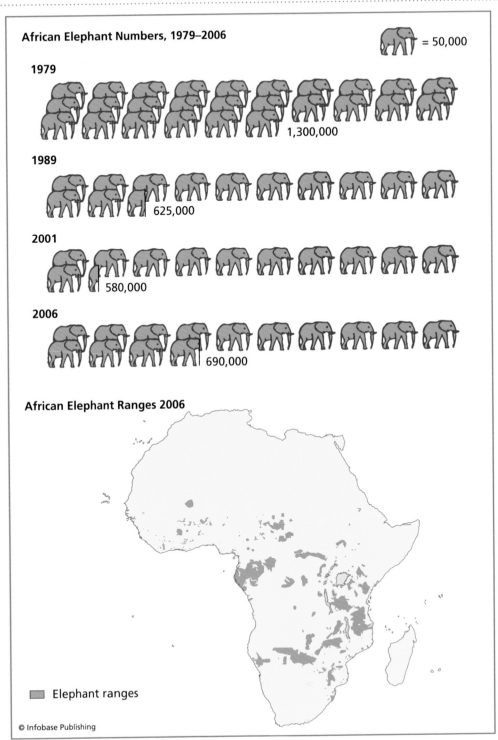

African Elephant Numbers, 1979–2006

= 50,000

1979

1,300,000

1989

625,000

2001

580,000

2006

690,000

African Elephant Ranges 2006

Elephant ranges

© Infobase Publishing

The Convention on International Trade in Endangered Species of Wild Fauna and Flora (CITES) has worked to protect plant and animal species internationally. One moderately successful program concerns the African elephants. Scientists estimate that there were 3 to 5 million African elephants at the beginning of the twentieth century. Two decades of poaching for their ivory tusks during the 1970s and 1980s brought numbers down from 1.3 million to 600,000. An ivory ban insti-

Rotting carcass of elephant killed by ivory poachers lying in the sun at Tsavo East Park. *(William F. Campbell / Time Life Pictures / Getty Images)*

tuted by CITES in 1989 reduced (but did not eliminate) poaching. Kenya has taken relatively good care of its elephants: The population was estimated at 167,000 in 1973, declined to 16,000 in 1989, and has rebounded to 27,000 today. Despite this progress, African elephants still face problems. Africa has a lot more fences than it did 100 years ago, and many elephant populations are no longer free to roam. Due to their large size, elephants eat a lot and are destructive, so they can wipe out a poor farmer's crop in one night. Limited hunting is now being allowed to cull the herds in some areas to save the farmers' livelihoods.

In 1973, the United States made a commitment to protect all animal and plant life threatened with extinction by passing the Endangered Species Act. The act has been very successful; only 9 of the more than 1,800 species on the list have been taken off due to extinction—

African elephant populations declined significantly in the 1970s because of habitat loss and unregulated poaching for the animals' valuable ivory tusks. A ban on ivory trading was introduced in 1989 so that the species would not become extinct. African elephant populations are now increasing at about 4% per year. All population numbers are just estimates.

a 99% success rate. Twenty-two of the listed species were removed because they have recovered, including the American peregrine falcon, Eggert's sunflower, the American alligator, the gray whale (which was removed from the list for part of its range), and (in July 2007) the bald eagle. The American crocodile may be downgraded to threatened because the population has recovered from 400 to more than 1,000, due primarily to restoration of its habitat in the Everglades.

SAVING SPECIES IN CAPTIVITY

If conservation of a threatened species in its natural habitat is not an option, or if there is a need to increase the genetic diversity of a species with only a small wild population, threatened or endangered species may be kept in a safe place such as a zoo or a botanical garden. Here the organisms can be managed in captive breeding programs designed to preserve their genetic diversity. Zoos interchange genetic material to increase the gene pool for these species. The ultimate aim of many of these programs is to return the species to its natural environment at some future, usually unknown, date.

With an epidemic raging through their wild populations, small and transportable amphibians are an obvious group to be sequestered in a zoo. As a last-ditch effort to save at least some species from extinction, curators from Zoo Atlanta and the Atlanta Botanical Garden have been flying to Panama to collect as many frogs as possible from groups that are dying out from infection by the chytrid fungus. These two facilities now contain more than 600 frogs from about 35 species; some are now the only survivors. The goal of this program is to maintain the frogs in captivity until the chytrid fungus can be eliminated in the wild. Newly collected frogs are given an antifungal bath before they are introduced into the collection, and the animals are not on display. The success of this program remains to be seen.

With only about 1,500 giant pandas left in the wild, and deforestation and poaching for skins a continual threat, captive breeding programs for these animals are thought to be an important source of new individuals. But until recently, captive pandas were rarely interested in mating. In 2006, though, China had the most panda cubs ever born in captivity: 31 in the first 10 months of the year (up from 12 in 2004 and nine in 2000). This success, officials say, was due to years of studying panda reproduction and to showing uninitiated males movies that illustrate the correct way of mating. Researchers are now trying to take this success to other countries where giant pandas reside in zoos.

SAVING SPECIES IN A FREEZER

Researchers at the San Diego Zoo have been saving the DNA of endangered species in their Frozen Zoo for over 25 years. The Frozen Zoo is the largest collection of genetic material from endangered species in the world, with over 7,200 individuals representing 675 species and subspecies. Frozen tissue from pandas, California condors, and a gray whale, among many others, are stored submerged and frozen in liquid nitrogen at a frigid -320°F (-196°C). The zoo is also a sperm bank that is used to improve the genetic diversity of rare species in captivity.

DNA from the Frozen Zoo has been used to clone endangered bantengs (also known as Bali cattle), which are found in small herds on the island of Java in Southeast Asia. The clones were created from a single skin cell taken from a captive banteng that died in 1980 before it was able to reproduce. The clone embryos were carried by ordinary beef cows. This technology may be useful in the future to introduce genetic diversity from long-dead animals into wild populations. At this time, relatively large quantities of tissue are needed, and the success rate is low. Only two of the original 30 banteng pregnancies went to term, and only one of the young survived. For these reasons, bringing back extinct animals is not technologically feasible at this time.

REINTRODUCING SPECIES INTO THE WILD

Species may be reintroduced into the wild from sequestered stock, such as that in a zoo, or they may be moved from a location in which they have a healthy population to a location where they are endangered or extinct. The most famous example of a reintroduction program is that of the California condor. The largest bird over North America, with a nearly 10-foot (3 m) wingspan, the condor is a holdover from the ice ages. Condor populations became so low, due to habitat loss and hunting, that the Los Angeles Zoo and the Peregrine Fund captured the remaining 22 birds in the 1980s. The condors then entered a captive breeding program designed to increase the number of young that each parent produced and the chances of survivability for each chick. Since 1992, over 140 condors have been released into remote portions of California, Arizona, and New Mexico, and many of the birds have reproduced successfully in the wild. Still, many condors have died, mostly from the lead poisoning they get from eating the lead-shot-riddled carcasses of animals that have been shot. With more than 130 condors flying over the southwestern skies, the program has been called a great success, although no one knows what its long-term prognosis will be.

Another type of reintroduction program takes a species that is thriving in one location to a location where it has gone extinct. This type of reintroduction is most commonly done with top predators that have been eradicated from all but the most wild and remote regions, but that are now desired (at least by some people) back in some of their original range. The Canadian lynx suffered great population losses in Colorado

Canadian Lynx have been moved from Canada, where they are thriving, to southwestern Colorado, where they had been extinct. So far, the reintroduction program has been successful. *(Terry Spivey, USDA Forest Service)*

between 1935 and 1972 (when the last known animal was trapped illegally) due to habitat loss and poisoning by farmers. Nearly 200 adult lynx relocated from the Canadian Yukon have been reintroduced into the San Juan Mountains of southwestern Colorado. The program is labeled a great success because the wild population is growing: The number of kittens that survive to reproductive age now exceeds the number of lynx that die each year. A program to reintroduce the lynx into the Adirondacks of the Northeastern United States in the 1980s failed when many animals were found as road kills.

WRAP-UP

Species can be saved in the wild, in captivity, or as tissue in a freezer. Frozen tissue saves the genetic material of one member of a species; that material may be used to enhance the genetic diversity of a wild or captive population or, at some time in the future, may be used to clone individuals of an extinct species. Live organisms in captivity are also repositories for genetic material. Some of these species are in captive breeding programs and may be reintroduced into the wild when conditions are more favorable. A species can also be reintroduced from a habitat where it is thriving into a habitat where it is endangered or extinct. By far, the best way to save biodiversity is to preserve the ecosystem in which the organism lives.

Preserving Lands

Setting aside land preserves biodiversity at all levels. Preserved lands can be virtually untouchable, or they can be used sustainably. National governments choose land for preservation, and the United Nations (UN) works internationally to call attention to ecosystems that are of global value and need protection. Important lands can be purchased by private organizations or individuals. Determining which lands should be targeted for preservation is controversial among conservation biologists: Some scientists measure biodiversity by species or genus, some measure by ecosystems, and some suggest preserving lands for the value of the ecosystem services they provide. Most conservation biologists agree that the urgency of the extinction problem requires that preservation take place where it can. The goal is to slow the rate of species extinction and, ultimately, to keep nature intact, with an extinction rate equal to that found in the absence of human influence.

NATIONAL LAND PROTECTION

Most countries have programs for protecting important ecosystems. Many have national parks: largely undeveloped lands that have been set aside by the government because they harbor exceptional native species and ecosystems, biodiversity, or beautiful natural landscapes. Kenya, with its incredible wildlife, relies on tourism for around 20% of its gross domestic product. To preserve this important resource, the Kenya Wildlife Service oversees an extensive network of national parks and much of the wildlife outside the parks.

While national parks are largely set aside for preservation, sustainable use is allowed in some preserved lands. **Extractive reserves** were first designed in the 1980s by rubber tappers in the Brazilian Amazon who wanted to preserve their livelihoods for the long term and so advocated sustainable use of the forest. Since then, the Brazilian government has set aside 25 extractive reserves, totaling more than 14,600 square miles (37,800 sq km) and benefiting approximately 45,000 people. Some Brazilian states have set aside their own extractive reserves. Although the amount of the Brazilian Amazon that is set aside in extractive reserves is currently only about 0.8%, the National Council of Rubber Tappers has a target of 10%. In extractive reserves, users must obtain permits for rubber tapping and for harvesting fruits, fish, chestnuts, oils, and other nontimber products. Cattle ranching, farming, and logging—activities that are destructive to the tappers' livelihoods—are generally not allowed. In one recently designated extractive reserve, three groups of nontraditional indigenous people are using dead wood to create furniture, which is sold in local markets and stores throughout Brazil. The people that depend on the reserve are hoping to begin selective and sustainable logging of 40 tree species.

Conserved lands in the United States have many different levels of protection. The strictest designation, the National Wilderness Preservation System (created under the Wilderness Act of 1964), sets aside lands that are exceptional and undisturbed. Only noninvasive activities such as fishing, hiking, and horseback riding are allowed, except in the vast spaces of Alaska, where motorized vehicles can be used. As of

March 2007, there were 702 wilderness areas in 44 of the 50 states plus Puerto Rico, preserving 107 million acres (433,000 sq km) and totaling about 2.5 percent of the entire United States.

Most wilderness areas are naturally beautiful, and some also have diverse ecosystems. In Alaska, the Noatak National Preserve and Gates of the Arctic Wilderness sets aside almost the entire watershed of the Noatak River—more than 6.5 million acres (260,000 sq. km) and the largest untouched river basin in America. In this region of superb natural beauty, moose, caribou, Dall sheep, wolves, lynx, and grizzly and black bears inhabit the forest, and native fish are found in the lakes and streams. Migratory birds hatch their young in the wilderness.

Since 1872, the year Yellowstone National Park was established in Wyoming, 58 national parks have been established in the United States. National parks are less restrictive than wilderness areas. Natural resources cannot be taken out of national parks, but the parks are often heavily used by tourists. National monuments are similar to national parks, but they usually contain only one unique resource each and are offered fewer protections.

Many national parks are set aside for their unusual geologic features and also for their important wildlife. Sequoia National Park, in California's beautiful Sierra Nevada mountains, protects Giant Sequoia trees, including the largest tree on the planet, the General Sherman tree (height: 274.9 feet [83.8 m]; diameter at base: 35.5 feet [11.1 m]; average crown spread: 106.5 feet [32.5 m]). A few national parks are purely biological resources. Everglades National Park sets aside 20% of the original wetland area of the Everglades. The Everglades has also been a World Heritage Site in Danger since 1993 due to nearby urbanization, nitrogen and mercury runoff, and flood protection measures that have caused water levels to fall. Hurricanes such as Andrew in 1992 and Katrina and Wilma in 2005 have also caused problems for the park's ecosystem. Everglades National Park is the only World Heritage Site in Danger in the United States, and the federal government has been working to correct some of these problems.

The U.S. Fish and Wildlife Service (FWS) manages the water and land of 545 National Wildlife Refuges on nearly 156,000 square miles

(405,000 sq km). Although the land is set aside for wildlife, hunting of some species is allowed on some refuges at some times. Tourism is an important source of income to the refuges and their surrounding areas, generating about $4 for every federal dollar spent. The largest is the Arctic National Wildlife Refuge (ANWR), with more than 30,000 square miles (78,000 sq km) of beautiful Alaskan wilderness crossing through tundra, taiga, and boreal forest biomes. The wildlife in the refuge is impressive, with 45 species of land and marine mammals, including Dall sheep, polar bears, grizzly bears, bowhead whales, moose, and caribou. The waters are home to 36 species of fish, and 180 species of birds have been sighted on refuge lands. Because the ANWR lies above oil reserves, its refuge status has been a source of contention in the United States Congress for decades.

The United States Forest Service (USFS) manages forests and grasslands for multiple uses, primarily logging, ranching, and recreation. The agency manages 300,000 square miles (780,000 sq km), an area the size of the state of Texas. Forest lands may be clear-cut or selectively logged; nowadays, most are reseeded so that the forest may grow again. The USFS recognizes the four greatest threats to U.S. forest lands—fire and fuel, invasive species, loss of open space, and unmanaged recreation—and is attempting to control these problems.

INTERNATIONAL PRESERVES

As an international body, the UN designates lands for protection as part of the United Nations Education, Scientific, and Cultural Organization (UNESCO). UNESCO protects natural and cultural resources as World Heritage Sites (WH) or as Biosphere Reserves. Most of these designations are on top of national designations already placed on the land.

World Heritage sites have been set up since 1972 to encourage the identification, protection, and preservation of cultural and natural heritages around the world. The sites include cultural treasures such as Stonehenge in the United Kingdom and Mesa Verde in Colorado, and natural treasures such as the Great Barrier Reef in Australia and the Grand Canyon in Arizona. Although these sites are said to belong to all of the world's people, the local people often are proud to be the guardians of an irreplaceable treasure.

The UNESCO Biosphere Reserves are land, coastal, or marine areas (or combinations thereof) that are set aside to preserve characteristic ecosystems. These ecosystems are managed for research and education as well as for protection; they allow the sustainable use of natural resources. At the core of a Biosphere Reserve is a region of no-use wilderness surrounded by buffer zones where research and selective economic exploitation are allowed. An example is the Mapimi Reserve in northeastern Mexico, where the endangered Bolson tortoise—North America's largest living land reptile, which was once hunted for meat—resides. Since the reserve was set up, in 1977, local residents have given up hunting but have become involved in research and environmental education. UN officials helped locals to develop more sustainable ranching practices and new sources of income, such as beekeeping.

One of the best known UNESCO sites is the Galapagos Islands and Marine Reserve, which has been a WH site since 1978 and a Biosphere Reserve since 1984. (The site was expanded in 2001.) The Reserve encompasses 97% of the land area of the Galapagos Islands and more than 10 times that area offshore. Tourists are attracted to the islands' rugged beauty and unusual species. Immigrants come from the mainland to work in the service industry at the tourist sites. All of these people, immigrants and tourists, require food and shelter and in return generate enormous amounts of waste. People have also brought alien species, including goats, which have decimated the islands' vegetation. The Ecuadoran government has instituted and enforced local protection for decades, and the UNESCO designations have added funding and safeguarding to their protections. UNESCO makes recommendations to the park, such as quarantine measures to reduce alien invasions, and has instituted a program to eliminate goats and other feral animals.

Locations on the UNESCO WH Site in Danger list include reserves that are under extraordinary pressure from the outside, such as the Everglades, described on page 150. The five WH sites in the

Marine iguanas (*Amblyrhynchus cristatus*) in the Galapagos Islands. These are the only lizards that live and forage in the sea. (*© Fritz Polking / The Image Works*)

Democratic Republic of Congo (DRC) in Africa give refuge to some of the last remaining mountain gorillas, northern white rhinos, and okapi. The DRC parks are in serious danger due to armed conflicts and civil strife. With nearly one million refugees living in Virunga Park, deforestation, poaching, and looting are out of control. In some parks, the staff has either fled or lacks the resources to do much. Because of their great biological resources, the UN, some governments, and nongovernmental organizations have pledged money and assistance to rehabilitate the DRC parks, and some progress is being made.

DO PARKS PROTECT ECOSYSTEMS AND SPECIES?

Parks are set aside to preserve a portion of an ecosystem, but they are not always effective. Some parks are not large enough for large animals to roam or do not have enough genetic diversity to maintain a healthy population. As human populations grow, and more people are interested in living near wild landscapes, development encroaches on the edges of parks. With development comes pressure from exotic species (from garden plants and pets, among others), pollution, and increased demand for energy and water. With the park nearby, more people visit; this requires more roads and results in more air pollution and more road kill. The greatest cause of death for the few remaining Florida panthers, for example, is collisions with vehicles.

Parks may preserve biodiversity locally, but conservationists are also concerned about preserving a variety of the world's ecosystems. To this end, participants in the Convention on Biological Diversity that took place in Rio de Janeiro in 1992 set the goal of preserving 10% of the planet's surface for biodiversity. This goal has been met on land, but the reality has not lived up to expectations. There is no global master plan, so the land set aside may not preserve many species or ecosystems. For example, the world's largest park, Greenland National Park, protects 375,000 square miles (972,000 sq km) of land but is mostly ice cap; this cold environment is home to only eight mammal species and no amphibians, freshwater turtles, or globally threatened birds. Countries may set aside land to meet their conservation targets, but there are no guidelines governing the lands they choose. The preserved land may be politically easier to set aside but not as biologically valuable as other land.

BUYING LAND

Conservationists agree that both governmental and market-based approaches are necessary to save biodiversity. Some environmental organizations use the political process to encourage governments to set aside lands, as when four environmental organizations spurred on the designation of 1.7 million acres (6,900 sq km) in southern Utah as the Grand Staircase-Escalante National Monument in 1996. Lands set aside by the government often benefit from some amount of private donation. The Great Smoky Mountains National Park exists only because of a five-million-dollar donation from John D.

Rockefeller Jr. and change collected by Depression-era schoolchildren in Knoxville, Tennessee.

Other organizations and individuals buy the land and maintain it themselves or donate it to a government or other agency. There are about 1,400 such land trusts in the United States. Land trusts have secured about 100,000 square miles (260,000 sq km) of land; some was previously farmed or developed and is being allowed to revert back to a natural state. One of the largest land trusts, The Nature Conservancy, has preserved over 50,000 square miles (83,000 sq km) around the world since its founding in 1951.

PRIORITIZING PRESERVATION

Individuals may save land that has appealed to them on some level as worth preserving. Organizations may look to save a certain landscape, ecosystem, or species. A few organizations (the UN, for example) take a broader approach, trying to preserve a variety of ecosystems; this is a challenge, given that money for conservation is limited. These organizations set priorities for what they want to preserve and then develop criteria for choosing which areas will best help them meet these priorities.

One strategy that has received a lot of attention from conservation biologists is the listing of **biodiversity hotspots**, an approach championed by Conservation International. This strategy attempts to preserve the greatest number of species with the smallest amount of money and effort. To be chosen as a hotspot, a location must have an incredible amount of biodiversity, which is assessed by tallying numbers of vertebrates and vascular plants. Most hotspots are in tropical rain forests, where species diversity is high, or on islands where there are many endemic species. Endemic species are given high priority because they are considered irreplaceable. To qualify as a hotspot, the area must also be experiencing enormous pressure. The region must have already lost at least 70% of its original natural vegetation and be at risk of losing more.

Using these criteria, Conservation International has identified 34 biodiversity hotspots. Although these lands cover only 2.3% of the

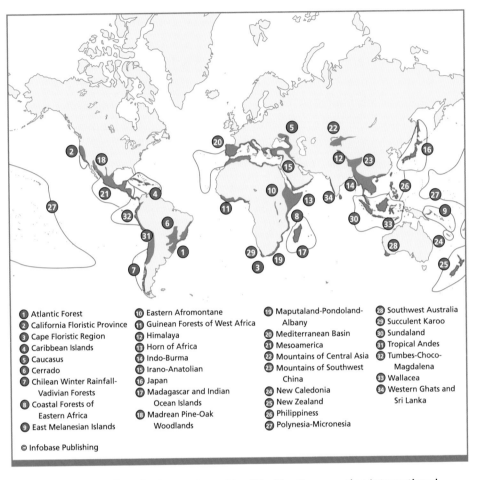

The world's 34 biodiversity hotspots, as identified by Conservation International. These hotspots were chosen for the numbers of species of plants and terrestrial vertebrates they contain in a small area.

Earth's surface, they harbor more than half of all plant species and 42% of all terrestrial vertebrate species. More than half of all known threatened species live in one of these biodiversity hotspots.

Many people support the biodiversity hotspot approach because it is straightforward and produces the most good for the least financial investment. But not all conservationists agree that the biodiversity hotspot approach is the best. By looking for the greatest species diversity, the program primarily preserves ecosystems in tropical and

Mediterranean climates, habitats that are largely in developing countries where people are accustomed to using their natural resources for their everyday needs. On the other hand, because such biomes as boreal forests and tundra have relatively low biodiversity, there is no hotspot in a boreal forest or tundra. There is only one biodiversity hotspot in the United States and one in Europe.

Some conservation biologists say that while biodiversity should be used to establish conservation priorities, genus is more important than species. These biologists argue that an extinct species with many close relatives in its genus has left more of its traits behind than an extinct species that was also the last of its genus. A biodiversity list of threatened genera differs greatly from one of endemic species. Kenya, for example, has relatively few endemic species but many unique and threatened genera, including eight highly threatened mammal genera: *Alcelaphus* (hartebeest), *Connochaetes* (gnu), *Hippotragus* (a type of antelope), *Oryx* (another type of antelope), *Otomops* (a type of bat), *Redunca* (reedbuck), *Rhynchocyon* (elephant shrew), and *Surdisorex* (mole shrew).

Rather than setting priorities on organisms, the World Wildlife Fund is choosing the most biologically diverse and representative terrestrial, freshwater, and marine habitats. Their Global 200 initiative suggests setting aside a broad variety of biologically rich habitats, ranging from the polar seas to coastal forests, tropical islands, and isolated deserts. Preserving these ecosystems would preserve a broad variety of endangered wildlife. The Global 200 list includes well-known sites such as Australia's Great Barrier Reef, the Galapagos Islands, and the Florida Everglades. Less well known are the Fynbos shrublands of South Africa, with their enormous plant diversity, and Indonesia's marine ecosystems, with their important coral reefs, turtles, sharks, and moray eels. Conservation International tries to correlate its biodiversity hotspots with the Global 200 list. There is a 92% overlap within the most crucial and endangered regions.

Another way to choose lands to preserve is to look at the value of the ecosystem services they provide. Although no wetlands make the biodiversity hotspots list because they generally have few endemic plants and are made up of relatively few species, wetlands are very valuable for their ecosystem services. The services they provide for flood regulation, waste treatment, and fisheries production total nearly $10,000 per hectare per year. (Tropical rain forests, although valuable, are valued at only $2,000 per hectare per year for their ecosystem services.)

Conservation International raised $750 million from private foundations and governments for its biodiversity hotspot program between 1990 and 2005. It is said to be the largest financial investment in any single conservation strategy. While no one would argue that this is not a step in the right direction, that money is only a small portion of the amount needed to preserve the 34 hotspots and countless future hotspots that might be added to the list. The estimated real cost is more than $2 billion.

RESTORING ECOSYSTEMS

Any conservationist will say that it is easier to preserve an ecosystem before it has been damaged or destroyed. But even if an ecosystem has been degraded by decades or even centuries of human abuse, it may still be worth preserving. Rebuilding ecosystems is the domain of **restoration ecology**, in which biologists assist the recovery of an ecosystem that has been degraded, damaged, or destroyed. The goals are to reestablish the biological community and ecosystem processes that were once native to the ecosystem and to set up the land for sustainable uses only.

The actions that restoration ecologists take depend on how disturbed the site is, what has disturbed it, and what it is currently used for. In some instances, the scientists need to perform only a single action; for example, removing a dam to reinitiate normal flooding. Alternatively, they may need to recreate all aspects of the ecosystem: its terrain, its water cycling, and its native plants and animals, for example. If a reference site is available, the scientists will study it to learn about its native species and ecological processes. They will then try to recreate that ecosystem in the damaged area by reintroducing native species and eliminating or controlling invasive species. After restoration, the biologists may allow the ecosystem to continue on its own, or they may need to manage the ecosystem, for example, to keep invasive species under control.

Ecosystem restoration must also take into account how much local people depend on the ecosystem. Where indigenous people are living sustainably with the land, they need to be supported; their knowledge can even be an important resource for restoration activities. But where the pressure to use the landscape unsustainably is high, local cultures must be taught to use the ecosystem in culturally appropriate and sustainable ways. Whatever action is taken, the relationship between the local people and the restored ecosystem must make sense in that context.

WRAP-UP

Preserving species and ecosystems will require multiple approaches. Biodiversity hotspots safeguard the greatest number of species of vascular plants and vertebrates for the smallest amount of land, which may correlate roughly with economic cost. But biodiversity hotspots mostly target tropical rain forests because of their enormous diversity and ignore other ways of measuring biodiversity. Looking at biodiversity by genus can put an umbrella of protection over other types of organisms. Looking at biodiversity by ecosystems, such as in the World Wildlife Fund's Global 200 program, can preserve a variety of ecosystems and, along with them, a variety of species. For there to be any chance of entering the twenty-second century with a large percentage of the biodiversity that was present at the beginning of the twenty-first, all possible approaches must be taken.

The Future of Biodiversity Conservation

This chapter describes actions that can be taken to preserve biodiversity. The first section focuses on the actions that a husband and wife team of tropical biologists has taken in the Area de Conservación Guanacaste (ACG) in Costa Rica to preserve tropical dry forest and the surrounding ecosystems. The team's philosophy is that ecosystems will be preserved when people recognize that biodiversity can provide what society wants. The second section is concerned with the contributions everyone can make to preserving biodiversity.

STRATEGIES OF BIOSPHERE CONSERVATION

Preserving ecosystems (or portions of them) outright is a very effective way to preserve biodiversity. This strategy works where the citizens are wealthy enough to allow land to be set aside simply for its aesthetic value, such as in North America. But in the developing world, there are too many people whose basic needs are not being met, or who desire a more comfortable standard of living, to allow lands to be set completely off limits. In addition, poachers, renegade loggers, and others who deplete the plants and animals are not easily deterred, and the national parks sometimes cannot afford the staff to keep out these lawbreakers.

Some conservation biologists think that the only way for an ecosystem in this circumstance to survive is for it to make at least some economic contribution to its human residents. This approach to preservation maintains the land's biodiversity in perpetuity and provides for the future of the people who depend on these resources.

AREA DE CONSERVACIÓN GUANACASTE

One location where biodiversity is being developed not only as a national park but also as a contributor to its community is the Area de Conservación Guanacaste (ACG) in northwestern Costa Rica, a region that contains 2.6% of the world's species. Behind this remarkable place is the work of two tropical biologists, Daniel Janzen and his wife, Winnie Hallwachs, both of the University of Pennsylvania. These American scientists and their Costa Rican colleagues are an example of what a group of people with extraordinary ideas and enormous dedication can do to preserve biodiversity. These scientists have used their knowledge in biology, politics, and economics to preserve a biologically diverse landscape that is as large as New York City and all of its suburbs.

In a 1998 essay in *Science*, titled "Gardenification of Wildland Nature and the Human Footprint," Janzen said, "The question is not whether we must manage nature, but rather how shall we manage it—by accident, haphazardly, or with the calculated goal of its survival forever?" According to Janzen, tropical forests are a "wildland garden," where there are thousands of "crops"—albeit crops to be harvested only when necessary for the wildland's survival as a essential part of society. These crops include ecotourism, biological education, biodiversity services, and ecosystem services, rather than the direct harvest of animals and plants. Janzen and his colleagues are "growing" these crops at ACG. As in any garden, human footprints can be found, but the art and science lies in minimizing the number of footprints and placing them where they do the least damage.

Half of ACG is in the tropical dry forest biome, which is among the most threatened forest ecosystems. Janzen believes that pristine Central American dry forest, containing species that have evolved to sustain a six-month annual drought, is now essentially gone. Over the past four centuries, it has been entirely fragmented and replaced by an agricultural landscape of fields, pastures, tree plantations, and urban sprawl.

Janzen knew that to create a healthy tropical dry forest ecosystem would require large, continuous tracts of land so that jaguars, mountain lions, and other large predators would have enough space to roam. With so much land, tens of thousands of smaller species would also have the geographic and ecosystem space they need to maintain healthy populations. Large and ecologically diverse tracts allow

Daniel Janzen and the ACG

Daniel Janzen was always a bit unusual. Although he collected bugs like many six year olds, he was still doing it as a ninth grader in 1953 when his father (who was the director of the U.S. Fish & Wildlife Service) asked him how the family should spend the two-month leave he had saved up from work. At Daniel's request, the family set out from their Minnesota home on a trip to Mexico to collect butterflies. When he discovered how much more wildlife diversity could be found in the tropics, the budding biologist was hooked. In graduate school, at a time when biology students tended to

do their field work close to home, Janzen chose to do his field work in Mexico, on the interaction between ants and the plants within which they live. Janzen continues to study animal-plant interactions by focusing on the caterpillars of moths and butterflies.

As a young Ph.D., Janzen followed a traditional path, becoming a professor at various universities before settling down at the University of Pennsylvania. He continued to do field work in tropical biology, primarily in northwestern Costa Rica. Over the years, Janzen saw development and degradation eating away species to recover from disastrous events such as fires, diseases, and climate change. Other ecosystems would also need to be included in the conservation area because many species of birds and insects migrate seasonally between the dry forest and the cloud and rain forests to the east. Janzen wanted the conserved wildland to be large enough to absorb human activities.

Meeting these goals would require a lot of land. Janzen and Hallwach's plan was to join together five small national parks and forest reserves by purchasing the private lands that lay between them. The scientists engineered the first large debt-for-nature swap. They arranged for the Swedish government to purchase some of Costa Rica's foreign debt; then Costa Rica's central bank paid a portion of the forgiven debt to the ACG in local currency. The scientists used the money to purchase the private lands and hire nearby residents as ACG staff. Over the years, Janzen and his colleagues have raised more than $50

at his field site as well as at conserved wildlands in the tropical parts of the world. Their awareness that tropical forests all over Latin America and the rest of the world were falling victim to bean fields and chainsaws led Janzen and his wife, Winnie Hallwachs, to decide to take whatever action they could to stop the destruction. In 1985, the couple joined with a group of Costa Ricans in both the private and government sectors to begin to piece together Area de Conservación Guanacaste (ACG). The Instituto Nacional de Biodiversidad (InBio) was formed soon after. Janzen and Hallwacks now live most of the year at ACG but spend the fall term teaching at the University of Pennsylvania.

Janzen is recognized as a worldwide leader in conservation biology. For his innovative work, the biologist has been awarded many prizes, including the Crafoord Prize (sometimes called the Nobel Prize of biology), a MacArthur "genius" award, and the 1997 Kyoto Prize in Basic Science (similar to Sweden's Nobel Prize). With the prize money, he has set up a trust for ACG, called the Guanacaste Dry Forest Conservation Fund, which raises funds for ACG land purchase and management.

million for the purchase and maintenance of ACG, most of which is now owned by the government of Costa Rica.

The private land that lay between the national parks was ranchland and low grade farmland, covered with thorny shrubs and dry grasses. Much of the land had not been forest for hundreds of years. The seeds from the native forest trees were long gone from the soil, but fragmented populations of trees persisted at the edges, in abandoned

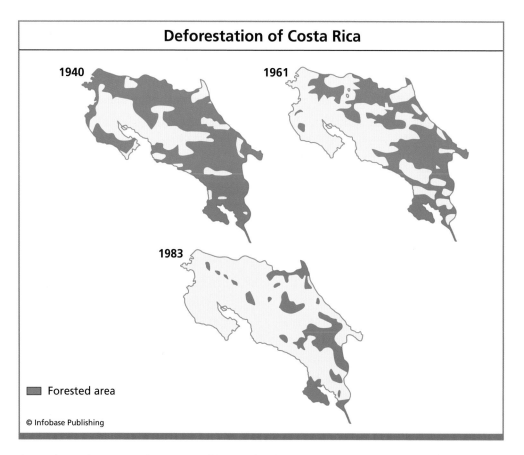

Deforestation of Costa Rica

1940

1961

1983

■ Forested area

© Infobase Publishing

Central American countries are small in size but large in population. Rapid population growth has depleted Costa Rica's rich forests because of building, farming, and cattle raising. This is a troublesome fact, as Costa Rica harbors a vast number of species, from plants, to mammals and birds, to insects. Through special projects, conservationists are working to replace the depleted forest areas and are concentrating on preserving the mountainous areas of land unsuitable for human living.

Restoration in the Area de Conservación Guanacaste in northwestern Costa Rica. The remaining tropical dry forest is being connected by restored ranchland that has been purchased for conservation. *(Photo courtesy Daniel Janzen)*

tracts, in ravines, and in other places that were protected from the annual fires set by locals to keep pastures clear. (There are no natural fires.) Invasive weeds were proliferating, and drainage patterns had been extensively altered. The soils had been compacted over many years by roaming cattle. The local culture accepted the status quo.

The forest needed (and continues to need) restoration. The forest fragments have mostly been left alone. No tree planting was necessary because birds, bats, and small terrestrial mammals, along with the winds, spread seeds to nearby areas. Human-caused fires were eliminated; without them, the woody vegetation has gradually taken over the pastures and old fields.

As of now, ACG consists of lands stretching from 12 miles (19 km) out in the Pacific Ocean in the west to well past the continental divide and into the Caribbean rain forest: 425 square miles (1,100 sq km) of land and 166 square miles (430 sq km) of ocean in all, or about 2% of Costa Rica. The landscape includes reefs, rivers, forests, and volcanoes. The dominant plant ecosystems are mangroves, swamps, dry forest, cloud and rain forests, and many kinds of intergrades between them. ACG has an estimated 235,000 species at a level greater than microbes, or about 2.6% of the world's biodiversity. Of these species, there are about 3,000 species of trees; 50,000 fungi; 950 vertebrates (140 species of mammals, over 300 species of birds, and 100 species of amphibians and reptiles); and over 100,000 species of insects, including about 130 species of Sphingidae moths. The most commonly seen large mammals are howler monkeys, white-faced capuchins, and white-tailed deer. There are also collared peccaries, five species of wild cats, ten species of hawks, and many other animals.

With land set aside and restoration in progress, four categories of "crops"—ecotourism, biological education, biodiversity services, and ecosystem services—are being harvested. The ongoing harvest of all of these crops is sustainable as long as it is organized, controlled, and structured with a full understanding of the organisms and ecosystems involved. The crops are as follows:

- ⊕ Ecotourism offers tourists the chance to experience the restoration of a tropical dry forest. Although the land is minimally developed for visitors, Costa Rican companies and guides take tourists into ACG, while services located nearby take care of them. The money that tourists bring with them helps support the local economy.

- ⊕ Education and research together are an important ACG crop. All local schoolchildren (approximately 2,500 per year) are brought to ACG to learn basic biology. This effort has produced a friendly array of neighbors (as has the fact ACG is the largest employer in the area) and will produce future leaders who understand both ACG and the ecology of the region. College and graduate students from within and outside Costa Rica come to ACG to take courses in field biology. They will become stewards of this and other conservation areas. ACG is also a major site for biological research, both basic and applied, by researchers around the world, an activity that brings several million dollars per year into the local economy.

⊕ Because of their amazing biodiversity, tropical forests harbor enormous potential for the development of pharmaceuticals and other products derived directly from wild plants, animals, fungi, and microbes. ACG staff members are generating a forest inventory and developing knowledge of these organisms so that they can be found, managed, and harvested in a nondamaging manner. Janzen and Rodrigo Gámez, a professor at the Universidad de Costa Rica, and a group of other Costa Ricans founded InBio with the mission to "support efforts to gather knowledge on the country's biological diversity and promote its sustainable use." InBio hires mostly Costa Ricans and is creating and managing a national inventory of all the living things of Costa Rica. Employees work with companies to find marketable products that can be taken sustainably from the forest.

⊕ With many tens of thousands of hectares of regenerating forest, ACG provides several ecosystem services. Each hectare will pull more than 200 metric tons of carbon out of the air over the coming decade, a large contribution toward reducing greenhouse gases. The ACG earns money to regenerate forests by providing companies the opportunity to pay management costs for this "biological air scrubber" to reduce their contributions to atmospheric greenhouse gases. Of equal importance, ACG forest produces water for several hundred thousand users in the surrounding agricultural landscape, water for urban dwellers, and possibly water for a large hydroelectric dam and irrigation projects.

As a result of innovative ideas, hard work, and the support of the Costa Rican government, ACG has been called the largest and most successful habitat restoration project in the world. In 1999, ACG was named a UNESCO World Heritage Site. Janzen sees ACG as a model for the revision of the entire Costa Rican national park system, forest service, and fish and wildlife service. ACG is now one of 11 similar projects at various stages of evolution that cover about 25% of the country.

POSITIVE STEPS TOWARD PRESERVING BIODIVERSITY

Not everyone can be the driving force behind saving a large piece of the planet's biodiversity. But there are other, smaller things that everyone can do to lessen his or her impact on biodiversity loss. A large contribution can be made by consuming less energy and fewer material products. Also important is to wisely choose the energy-consumption and material products one uses. Following are some small actions everyone can take in his or her daily life:

- Reduce, Reuse, Recycle: This old slogan embodies three ways to lessen our impact on the planet's biodiversity. Reducing consumption is by far the best: Trees will not be felled for furniture or paper not purchased; oil will not be pumped for cars that are not driven, and unused cars do not cause pollution. Reusing products is a more efficient use of material; for example, using both sides of a piece of paper. Recycling materials uses less energy and much less material than manufacturing a new product. Recycling a milk jug is much less wasteful than throwing it in the landfill. (Even better is using refillable milk bottles.) Buying recycled products saves on materials and energy and encourages industry to buy recycled materials, which in turn encourages communities to recycle.
- Walk or bike whenever possible: When buying a car, choose one that is energy efficient, and look into new technologies, such as hybrid cars, that use less energy.
- Be an educated consumer: When buying new products, choose wood and paper items that are harvested from sustainably managed forests. Look for the Forest Stewardship

Council logo, or visit the council's Web site to find stores that carry these products. Look for products that do not exploit the biodiversity hotspots. If using a product such as ginseng, be sure that the plant is cultivated, not taken from the wild.

⊕ Avoid buying exotic pets. Exotic animals did not evolve for a human environment, and they do not make good pets. Instead, adopt one of the multitude of domesticated animals that need homes. If an exotic pet must be purchased, be sure to choose one that is bred in captivity. Check the information from the Marine Aquarium Council (listed in the For Further Reading section of this book) before stocking an aquarium, to find out which species are harvested or farmed sustainably and which are not.

⊕ Never dump unwanted animals or plants. Do not set birds or the contents of aquariums free.

⊕ Be an educated traveler. Be aware that there are many items that travelers are not allowed to import into the United States, and that there are some products that are not yet banned but perhaps should be. For guidance, travelers should carry with them downloadable Buyer Beware guides or the clip-and-save list of products put out by TRAFFIC. If possible, support ecotourism.

⊕ Band together with others to preserve biodiversity by donating money or time to organizations that buy or lobby to preserve lands and marine locations. Make a donation to purchase land for ACG or other, similar, regions. Donations from kids in 22 countries helped establish the Children's Eternal Rain Forest in Costa Rica, where more than 54,000 acres (22,000 hectares) have been preserved since 1989.

⊕ Promote biodiversity at home. Plant native vegetation, and pull down fences to allow wildlife to visit. Avoid using plants that could become invasive species.

⊕ Become educated politically. Lobby representatives to create and enforce environmentally sound policies locally, nationally, and internationally.

- ⊕ Encourage businesses and organizations to consider the long-term effects of their actions. In your private life and when taking part in business decisions, add in the environmental costs of any action before pursuing it.
- ⊕ Think globally. Be aware of the problems faced by people in other countries, and make choices that will help them to live in harmony with their natural environment.
- ⊕ Check out the many suggestions for preserving biodiversity on Conservation International's Web site, which is listed in the For Further Reading section of this book.

WRAP-UP

Habitats are being lost at a tremendous rate worldwide, but individuals can have less of an impact on the environment by consciously choosing to buy less and to buy products that are harvested sustainably. Fortunately, people such as Daniel Janzen and Winnie Hallwachs are working to save or restore important ecosystems to conserve biodiversity. By integrating ACG into the community and using it to supply jobs to residents, both the local people and the government of Costa Rica are motivated to preserve the landscape for all time.

Conclusion

The diversity of life on the Earth is absolutely astonishing. Organisms have adapted ways to live in nearly all of the conditions found on the planet. Microbes inhabit rock 2 miles (3 km) deep inside the Earth's crust; small invertebrates are found in the deepest ocean; and monkeys swing through the rain forest canopy far above the ground. Perhaps even more amazing are the complex connections between organisms and their environments that make up the planet's various ecosystems. Coral animals build reefs that support a multitude of fish and invertebrates; tropical rain forests sustain a three-dimensional world of plants and animals with the greatest biodiversity on Earth; tundra plants survive for long months of winter darkness in the frigid cold and wind. The theory of evolution explains how all species become adapted to live in and be an important member of an ecosystem.

Extinction has also been essential for the development of life on Earth. Over geologic time, multitudes of species have gone extinct because they could not adapt fast enough to the changing environment.

At least five times in the planet's history, a large percentage of species were extinguished at the same time. After these mass extinction events, life was very different than it was before because new organisms evolved to fill the abandoned niches. Such a switch took place 65 million years ago, when an asteroid impact propelled the planet from the Age of Reptiles, when dinosaurs and other reptiles filled most major niches, to the Age of Mammals, when mammals evolved different strategies for filling those same niches. In this way, mass extinctions have changed the course of evolution.

Many biologists say that the Earth is at the cusp of a new mass extinction, the sixth. Unlike the others, this extinction is being caused by one of the planet's species. As humans alter the environment to better suit our interests, the species extinction rate has accelerated to between 10 and 100 times over what would be normal. The largest damage is done as vast amounts of land are logged, bulldozed, plowed, burned, and paved over to make way for homes, farms, ranches, mines, industrial complexes, and other human landscapes. Remaining habitats are fragmented or become degraded by pollution. Hunting and fishing take a direct toll on biodiversity: Some ocean fisheries have collapsed, and others are being seriously overfished. Rain forest animals in Africa and Southeast Asia are falling prey to the bushmeat trade, and many species, including all six of the nonhuman great apes, are threatened or endangered. Threatened and endangered plants and animals are also gathered for medicines, exotic pets, and luxury items. As ecosystems are being pressured from outside, invasive species are moving in. While many integrate well into the native ecosystem, a few completely alter it. Perhaps the worst example is the Australian brown tree snake, which has devoured most of the native bird species of Guam. Damage to biodiversity also comes from global sources, as climate change affects ecosystems. For example, global warming seems to have joined together with a bacterial pathogen to wipe out many species of frogs and toads.

Biodiversity is suffering for a number of reasons. In developed countries, overconsumption is largely to blame. It seems that there are always more people wanting to live more comfortable lives. Many ecosystems in developed nations have already been destroyed or damaged: Nearly all of the forests in the United States have been logged, and many wetlands have been drained.

The search for resources has taken the developed nations to developing countries, where forests are being felled for timber to meet the developed nations' demands. Japan, for example, with little forest of its own, relies on wood from Southeast Asian forests. Ranches in the Brazilian Amazon supply beef to fast-food restaurants in North America and Europe. Besides supplying products for the wealthier nations, developing countries alter land for farming or ranching by their own people.

Although the rate at which ecosystems are being lost is high, efforts are being made to preserve some of the planet's biodiversity. Organisms are best saved in their native habitats, but when that is not possible, or when their genetic diversity in the wild needs to be supplemented, their genes may be preserved as individual species in a zoo or as tissue in a freezer. Zoos are now the home of last resort for some tropical frog and toad species, as many are being lost in the wild to a global epidemic. Rarely, a species present only in captivity is rereleased into the wild, as was done with the California condors that now fly over some of the remote regions of the desert Southwest. Scientists hope that captive breeding of the amphibians will lead to their being let back into the wild when the epidemic passes.

National parks and preserves can be set aside to protect biodiversity. In these areas, the land is free from habitat destruction but not from pollution. No national park boundary can stop pesticide residue and car exhaust from entering Yosemite National Park in California, for example.

Even parks that are so isolated that they are free from pollutants can be affected by human activities. In fact, no region on Earth can escape the changes being wrought by global warming. Costa Rica's Monteverde Cloud Forest sits on top of a mountain, protected from development and pollution. Yet warmer temperatures have changed conditions in the park and allowed a pathogen to go out of control, wiping out the endemic Monteverde golden toad. If an isolated park in an ecologically sensitive country does not protect the species within it, how effective are parks? The answer is, no one knows; but parks are one important means to maintain biodiversity.

In many nations, wildlands can be preserved only if they make an economic contribution to the community. The "crops" these lands provide must be harvested sustainably so that the people who depend on the land can continue to benefit from it while the biodiversity remains preserved. Costa Rica's ACG is the beacon example of a wildland that is being restored and preserved with these long-term goals. The cost so far is upwards of $50 million and countless hours of human effort, but ACG contributes immeasurably to the local community and the biosphere.

The question that has not yet been answered is whether biodiversity should be saved. The reasons for preserving biodiversity are practical: They include maintaining the availability of resources, ecosystem services, and the possibility of finding compounds for pharmaceuticals and other products. There are aesthetic reasons as well—reasons that involve the planet we want people of the future to be a part of.

To protect biodiversity for people who are alive today and for their children, much of what is left of pristine ecosystems should be preserved, particularly in the developed nations where little remains. Degraded and destroyed land should be restored, especially if it is the only habitat of its kind remaining. Species should be preserved in parks and, as a last resort, in zoos. Climate change, which is really the great unknown, must be dealt with head on. For the rate of global warming to be slowed, a concerted effort must be made by all nations to find alternative energy sources and to make energy conservation a part of people's everyday lifestyles.

The important changes in how humans use resources and preserve wildlands will be made on a large scale only when young people get involved. After all, it is the future of the young—and their children, and their children's children—that is being compromised as biodiversity is lost. The work to preserve biodiversity is fundamental to our survival and cannot be put off much longer.

Appendix

The organisms listed below are among those mentioned in the text of this volume. Where possible, the organism's scientific name is given as genus and species. In some cases, there is more than one species that the text could be referring to, so the genus name is given followed by *sp* (e.g., *Pinus* sp.). In other cases, the text refers to a specific sub-species of the organism, so that is listed (e.g., *Bufo boreas boreas*).

Organism

FUNGUS

Pine blister rust

PLANTS

Aloe
American ginseng
American sycamore
Asian ginseng
Australian melaleuca tree
Bigleaf scurfpea (extinct)
Brazil nut
Brazilian pepper
Coastal redwood
Douglas fir
Eggert's sunflower
Fir
Flowering dogwood
Foxglove
Giant sequoia

Scientific name

Cronartium ribicola

Aloe vera
Panax quinquefolius
Platanus occidentalis
Panax ginseng
Melaleuca quinquenervia
Orbexilum macrophyllum
Bertholletia excelsa
Schinus terebinthifolius
Sequoia sempervirens
Pseudotsuga menziesii
Helianthus eggertii
Abies sp.
Cornus florida
Digitalis sp.
Sequoiadendron giganteum

Jeffrey pine	*Pinus jeffreyi*
Loblolly pine	*Pinus pinus taeda*
Milfoil	*Myriophyllum spicatum*
Pacific yew tree	*Taxus brevifolia*
Paper birch	*Betula papyrifera*
Piñon pine	*Pinus* sp.
Ponderosa pine	*Pinus ponderosa*
Quaking aspen	*Populus tremuloides*
Red maple	*Acer rubrum*
Restharrow	*Ononis alopecuroides*
Rubber tree	*Hevea brasiliensis*
Saguaro	*Carnegiea gigantea*
Sapucaia	*Lecythis* sp.
Silk-cotton	*Ceiba pentandra*
Spruce	*Picea* sp.
Western hemlock	*Tsuga heterophylla*
White pine	*Pinus strobus*

INSECTS

Apollo (butterfly)	*Parnassius apollo*
Monarch (butterfly)	*Danaus plexippus*
Mountain pine beetle	*Dendroctonus ponderosae*
Piñon bark beetle	*Ips confusus*
Plain tiger (butterfly)	*Danaus chrysippus*
Purple emperor (butterfly)	*Apatura iris*

INVERTEBRATES

Giant tubeworm	*Riftia pachyptila*
Horseshoe crabs	*Limulus polyphemus*
Rosy periwinkle	*Catharanthus roseus*
Zebra mussel	*Dreissena polymorpha*

FISH

Alaska pollock	*Theragra chalcogramma*
Cod	*Gadus* sp.

Coelacanth	*Latimeria chalumnae*
Chilean sea bass	*Dissostichus eleginoides*
Flying fish	*Cypselurus* sp.
Mackerel	*Scomberomorus* sp.
Mekong giant catfish	*Pangasius gigas*
Perch	*Perca* sp.
Piranha	*Pygocentrus* sp.
Sea lamprey	*Petromyzon marinus*
Swordfish	*Xiphias gladius*
Tilapia	*Tilapia* sp.
Tuna	*Thunnus* sp.

AMPHIBIANS

Boreal toad	*Bufo boreas boreas*
Harlequin frog	*Atelopus varius*
Jambato toad	*Atelopus ignescens*
Monteverde golden toad	*Bufo periglenes*
Red-eared slider turtle	*Trachemys scripta elegans*

REPTILES

American alligator	*Alligator mississippiensis*
American crocodile	*Crocodylus acutus*
Anaconda	*Eunectes murinus*
Australian brown tree snake	*Boiga irregularis*
Bolson tortoise	*Gopherus flavomarginatus*
Green iguana	*Iguana iguana*
Marine iguana	*Amblyrhynchus cristatus*
Nile monitor lizard	*Varanus niloticus*
Python	*Python* sp.
Water monitor lizard	*Varanus mertensi*

BIRDS

American peregrine falcon	*Falco peregrinus anatum*
Arctic tern	*Sterna paradisaea*
Bald eagle	*Haliaeetus leucocephalus*

Blackburnian warbler	*Dendroica fusca*
Blackcap	*Sylvia atricapilla*
Blue-and-yellow macaw	*Ara ararauna*
California condor	*Gymnogyps californianus*
Canary	*Serinus canaria*
Chifchaff	*Phylloscopus collybita*
Crow	*Corvus* sp.
Dodo (extinct)	*Raphus cucullatus*
Emperor penguin	*Aptenodytes forsteri*
European starling	*Sturnus vulgaris*
Golden eagle	*Aguila chrysaetos*
Hawaiian rail (extinct)	*Porzana sandwichensis*
Hyacinth macaw	*Anodorhynchus hyacinthinus*
Koko (Guam rail)	*Rallus owstoni*
Northern spotted owl	*Strix occidentalis caurina*
Parakeets	*Psittacula* sp.
Passenger pigeon (extinct)	*Ectopistes migratorius*
Peregrine falcon	*Falco peregrinus*
Pied flycatcher	*Ficedula hypoleuca*
Ptarmigan	*Lagopus muta*
Red-crowned parrot	*Amazona viridigenalis*
Roseate spoonbill	*Platalea ajaja*
Rufous hummingbird	*Selasphorus rufus*
Snowy owl	*Bubo scandiacus*
Spix's macaw	*Cyanopsitta spixii*
Whitethroat	*Sylvia communis*

MAMMALS

African pygmy mouse	*Mus minutoides*
Amazonian manatee	*Trichechus inunguis*
Amazon River dolphin	*Inia geoffrensis*
American bison (buffalo)	*Bison bison*
Baboon	*Papio* sp.
Banteng (Bali cattle)	*Bos javanicus*
Bighorn sheep	*Ovis* canadensis

Black bear	*Ursus americanus*
Black rat	*Rattus rattus*
Black-tailed deer	*Odocoileus hemionus columbianus*
Bowhead whale	*Balaena mysticetus*
Brazilian tapir	*Tapirus terrestris*
Canadian lynx	*Lynx canadensis*
Capuchin monkey	*Cebus* sp.
Capybara	*Hydrochoerus hydrochaeris*
Cat (domestic)	*Felis silvestris catus*
Caribou (Reindeer)	*Rangifer tarandus*
Caribbean monk seal (extinct)	*Monachus tropicalis*
Cheetah	*Acinonyx jubatus*
Chimpanzee	*Pan troglodytes*
Collared peccary	*Tayassu tajacu*
Cougar	*Puma concolor*
Dall sheep	*Ovis dalli*
Dog (domestic)	*Canus lupus familiaris*
Elephant (African)	*Loxodonta* sp.
Elephant (Asian)	*Elephas maximus*
Elephant seal	*Mirounga* sp.
Elk	*Cervus elaphus*
Finback whale	*Balaenoptera physalus*
Florida panthers	*Puma concolor coryi*
Gambian giant pouched rat	*Cricetomys gambianus*
Giant panda	*Ailuropoda melanoleuca*
Giraffe	*Giraffa camelopardalis*
Gray whale	*Eschrichtius robustus*
Grizzly bear	*Ursus arctos horribilis*
Guadalupe fur seal	*Arctocephalus townsendi*
Guinea pig (domestic)	*Cavia porcellus*
Hare/rabbit	*Lepus* sp.
Hippopotamus	*Hippopotamus amphibius*
Howler monkey	*Alouatta* sp.
Human	*Homo sapiens sapiens*

Jaguar	*Panthera onca*
Kangaroo	*Macropus* sp.
Koala	*Phascolarctos cinereus*
Lion	*Panthera leo*
Macaque	*Macaca* sp.
Manatee	*Trichechus* sp.
Marmoset	*Callithrix* sp.
Moose	*Alces alces*
Mountain gorilla	*Gorilla beringei beringei*
Musk deer	*Moschus* sp.
Musk ox	*Ovibos moschatus*
Northern elephant seal	*Mirounga angustirostris*
Nutria	*Myocaster coypus*
Ocelot	*Leopardus pardalis*
Okapi	*Okapia johnstoni*
Pangolin	*Manus* sp.
Pika	*Ochotona* sp.
Platypus	*Ornithorhynchus anatinus*
Polar bear	*Ursus maritimus*
Prairie dog	*Cynomys* sp.
Pronghorn antelope	*Antilocapra americana*
Puma	*Leopardus pardalis*
Raccoon	*Procyon* sp.
Red fox	*Vulpes vulpes*
Rhesus monkey	*Macaca mulatta*
Saiga antelope	*Saiga tatarica*
Sea otter	*Enhydra lutris*
Siberian tiger	*Panthera tigris altaica*
Spider monkey	*Ateles* sp.
Squirrel monkey	*Saimiri sciureus*
Steller's sea lion	*Eumetopias jubatus*
Sumatran rhinoceros	*Dicerorhinus sumatrensis*
Three-toed sloth	*Bradypus* sp.
Tiger	*Panthera tigris*
Vampire bat	*Desmodus rotundus*

Wallaby	*Macropus* sp.
West Indian manatee	*Trichechus manatus*
White-faced capuchin	*Cebus capucinus*
White-footed mouse	*Peromyscus leucopus*
White rhinoceros	*Ceratotherium simum*
White-tailed deer	*Odocoileus virginianus*
Wolf	*Canis lupus*
Woodchuck	*Marmota momax*
Woolly monkey	*Lagothrix* sp.
Zebra	*Equus* sp.

Glossary

adaptation   A structure or behavior alteration that is inheritable; that is, able to be passed from one generation to the next.

aerobic   An environment containing oxygen, or an organism that breathes oxygen.

air pollution   Contamination of the air by particulates and toxic gases in concentrations that can endanger human and environmental health. Also known as smog.

algae   A very diverse group of organisms that make up a portion of two different kingdoms; they are not plants, although some look like plants, and all photosynthesize.

alien species   Organisms that are introduced by human activities into a location where they are not native; marine invasive species often travel in the ballast water of ships.

allele   Alleles are different DNA codings that occupy the same locus on the same chromosome; they are different forms of the same gene.

amino acids   Simple organic molecules containing carbon, hydrogen, oxygen, nitrogen, and sometimes sulfur; amino acids are the building blocks of proteins.

anaerobic   An oxygen-free environment or an organism, such as a bacterium, that lives in an oxygen free environment.

angiosperm   Seed plants that cover their seeds in a true fruit, with reproductive organs in a structure called a flower.

arthropods   Animals with a segmented body covered by an exoskeleton; most of the planet's arthropods are insects, but other arthropods include spiders, crabs, lobsters, and shrimp.

artificial selection   Humans perform artificial selection to bring about changes in a species of organisms. Artificial selection has given rise to the multiple breeds of dogs that are present today.

asteroid   A rock or tiny planet that orbits the Sun, sometimes colliding with another asteroid, a moon, or a planet; an asteroid impact has been blamed for the mass extinction of the dinosaurs and other species 65 million years ago.

atmosphere   The gases surrounding a planet or moon.

bacteria   Microscopic, single-celled organisms that live in an incredible diversity of environments.

bioaccumulation   The accumulation of toxic substances within living organisms.

biocontrol   Biological control; using a predator or a pest species to control the population of an unwanted organism, such as an invasive species.

biodiversity   The number of species in a given habitat.

biodiversity hotspot   An ecosystem chosen for protection due to its high biodiversity and the risk that all of it will soon be lost; Conservation International maintains a list of biodiversity hotspots that currently contains 34 hotspots.

biomass   The mass of all the living matter in a given area or volume of a habitat.

biome   Individual ecosystem that contains similar climate and life within its area; examples of some biomes include tundra, tropical rain forest, and desert.

biosphere   All of Earth's living creatures.

boreal forest   Frigid biome of northern Eurasia and Canada, dominated by fir trees and diverse mammal life; snow is the dominant precipitation.

bushmeat　The meat of wild animals hunted for commercial purposes.

canopy　The dense ceiling of a forest, created by the tops of the main body of trees; the largest percentage of the plants and animals of the tropical rain forest live in the canopy.

carnivore　An animal that eats other animals.

cell　The smallest unit of structure and function making up all living things; a life form may be composed of one cell or of many trillions of cells, as in humans and other complex organisms.

cetaceans　Marine mammals that include whales, dolphins, and porpoises.

chemosynthesis　The creation of food energy by breaking down chemicals. Chemosynthetic organisms are found only at hydrothermic vents.

chlorofluorocarbon (CFC)　A man-made gas that rises into the stratosphere and breaks down ozone molecules.

comet　A celestial body made of rocks, ice, and gases that orbits the Sun.

consumer　An organism that feeds on other plants or animals for food energy.

crustaceans　Mostly marine members of the phylum Arthropoda; crustaceans include lobsters, crabs, and shrimp.

data　Facts that may be used as evidence to create a hypothesis or theory.

DDT (dichlorodiphenyltrichloroethane)　A toxic chemical; DDT was a very effective insecticide but was withdrawn from production when its negative effects (and those of its breakdown products) on birds and mammals were realized.

dead zone　An ocean region that is hostile to most life, usually due to eutrophication.

deciduous　Word used to describe trees that lose their leaves in the winter to avoid freezing or in the dry season to avoid desiccation; deciduous forests are made mostly of deciduous trees.

decomposer   An organism that breaks down the body parts of dead organisms or their waste into nutrients that can be used by other plants and animals.

deforestation   The conversion of forest area to nonforest area, often agricultural land or settlements.

desert   Biome with hot, dry summers and low annual precipitation. Desert plants and animals are well adapted to conserving water and keeping cool; cacti are among the most unusual desert plants.

DNA (deoxyribonucleic acid)   The nucleic acid that carries hereditary information from parent cell to daughter cell. When a cell divides, its DNA makes an identical copy of itself that is passed to its daughter.

dry forest   A tropical or subtropical forest in which a great deal of rain falls each year but in which there is also a long annual drought, up to eight months.

echinoderms   The group of marine organisms that attach to the seafloor and that include sea stars, brittle stars, sea urchins, sand dollars, and sea cucumbers.

ecology   The study of the distribution and abundance of species and their relationship to their environments.

ecosystem   The interrelationships among the plants and animals of a region and the raw materials that they need to live.

ectotherm   An animal whose body temperature is the same as its surrounding environment; also called "cold blooded."

ecotourism   Tourism that is environmentally and culturally sensitive. Ideally, ecotourism is sustainable; brings a source of income into the region; and educates the tourists on the political, environmental, and social climate of the region and the country.

embryo   A young organism during the time between fertilization and the point at which the organism is structurally complete and can survive as an individual.

endangered species   An organism that is threatened with extinction.

endemic species   A species that is found only in a particular location, such as on an island.

endotherm   An animal that uses food energy to fuel its body temperature, which remains nearly constant without being affected by the temperature of its environment; also called "warm-blooded."

estuary   The location where a river meets the sea and where there is great variability in salinity and a rich habitat for diverse organisms.

eukaryote   A cell with a nucleus bound by a membrane and with genetic material organized into chromosomes; a eukaryotic cell can be an entire organism, or many eukaryotic cells can come together to make an organism.

eutrophication   The changes that occur in an aquatic ecosystem when excessive nutrients are released; the term is used commonly to refer to the depletion of oxygen by bacteria.

evapotranspiration   The loss of water by evaporation from plants.

evergreen   Word used to describe trees and shrubs that have green leaves or needles year round and that shed them only when new growth appears; evergreen forests are made primarily of evergreen trees.

evolution   Change through time. In science, evolution usually refers to organic evolution, which is the change in organisms through time by the process of natural selection.

extinction   A species is extinct if no member survives and reproduces. This can occur in two ways: In the first example, the species cannot evolve to keep up with a changing environment; it dies out, and its genes are lost. In the second example, the species evolves into another species, and its most useful genes are preserved.

extractive reserve   Preserved land in which a few resources are allowed to be taken; Brazil has set up extractive reserves at the request of rubber tappers.

flood basalt   A giant volcanic eruption that coats the land surface with fluid lava that may emit gases and particles on such a massive scale that a mass extinction occurs.

food chain A chain that tracks food energy from producer to primary consumer to secondary consumer and so on, ending with decomposers.

food web Overlapping food chains that form a web that makes up the biological portion of an ecosystem.

fossil fuels Ancient plants that have decayed and been transformed into a useable fuel, especially coal and petroleum. These fuels are really just stored ancient sunshine.

fungi Single or multicellular heterotrophs that absorb nutrients into their cells from living or dead plant or animal tissues; fungi include yeasts, molds, and mushrooms.

gene The unit of inheritance that passes a trait from one generation to the next.

gene pool The sum of all the genes in the population of a given species.

global warming The worldwide rising of average global temperature; the term usually refers to the temperature increases that have taken place in the past one-and-a-half centuries.

greenhouse gases Gases that absorb heat radiated from the Earth. They include carbon dioxide, methane, ozone, nitrous oxide, and chlorofluorocarbons.

gymnosperm Woody, vascular plant that uses seeds for reproduction; conifers and ginkgos are gymnosperms.

habitat An environment in which an organism lives, with distinctive features such as climate, resource availability, predators, and many others.

habitat fragmentation The breaking apart of a continuous habitat by humans due to the conversion of some of the land to other uses, such as agriculture or development.

heavy metal A metal with high weight, especially one that is toxic to organisms.

herbivore Plant-eating animals that make up the second level of a food web (the first level of consumers).

homologous structures Structures in different species that are modifications of a structure from a common ancestor; vertebrate forelimbs are homologous; examples include bat and bird wings and amphibian legs.

human overkill hypothesis The hypothesis that humans hunt many animals to extinction shortly after arriving in a new region.

hydrocarbon An organic compound composed of hydrogen and carbon; fossil fuels are hydrocarbons.

hydrothermal vent A hot spring on the seafloor, usually found along a mid-ocean ridge, where extremely hot water meets frigid seawater and precipitates metallic minerals.

hypothesis An explanation for a set of data that may be verified or disproved by further information.

indigenous Originating in, and characteristic of, a particular region or country; native.

invasive species Organisms that are introduced by human activities into a location where they are not native; marine invasive species often travel in the ballast water of ships.

invertebrate An animal without a backbone; sponges, jellies, clams, spiders, coral, and lobsters are all examples of invertebrates.

jungle Thick forest understory where the rain forest canopy has been disturbed, allowing more light than normal to enter.

kelp Tall, fast-growing seaweeds.

keystone species A species of plant or animal that is crucial to the health of the entire community; often a top carnivore.

law An explanation of events that occur with unvarying uniformity under the same set of circumstances.

life Living things can be distinguished from nonliving things by their organization, metabolism, growth, irritability, adaptation, and reproduction. These functions are performed by single-celled organisms and by complex organisms with multiple organs and systems.

limiting factor   A physical or biological factor (for example, a nutrient or light) that restricts the number of individuals of a species that exist in a given area.

mangrove   A flowering tree that grows in dense forests along tropical shorelines and has its roots submerged for part of the day; mangrove ecosystems perform many important environmental services.

marine reserves   Marine reserves are more restrictive than marine protected areas. Reserves are "no take," meaning that no resources of any sort may be harvested.

marsh   Low wetland, often treeless but covered with grasses, periodically covered with water

mass extinction   An event during which 25% or more of the planet's species go extinct in a relatively short period of time; a mass extinction opens many ecological niches that need to be filled and so is a driving force of evolution.

mercury   The only metal that is liquid at room temperature. It is toxic in liquid form and also as a salt or an organic compound.

metabolism   The sum of all the biochemical processes necessary for life, including the building up or breaking down of complex organic molecules from simpler substances.

mollusks   Invertebrates with an internal or external shell; mollusks include clams, snails, abalones, limpets, octopuses, and squid.

mutation   A random change in a gene that may be beneficial, harmful, or neutral to the success of the individual and species.

natural selection   The mechanism that drives organic evolution. Natural processes affect the reproductive success of an organism, which steers the way a species will evolve.

niche   The role an organisms fills in its ecosystem; a particular species of bird may fill the niche of small flying creature with a long bill that can sip nectar from a particular species of flower.

nucleic acids   Substances found in chromosomes and in viruses that are central to the storage and replication of hereditary information and the expression of this information through protein synthesis; The two main types of nucleic acids are DNA, which carries hereditary information from parent to daughter, and RNA, which delivers this information to the sites where cells manufacture proteins.

nucleus (1) The "brains" of a cell, the part that directs the cell's important functions. (2) The center of an atom, composed of protons and neurons.

nutrients Biologically important elements that are critical to growth or to building shells or bones; nitrates, phosphorous, carbonate, and silicate are some nutrients needed by marine organisms.

old-growth forest Forest containing trees that have never been logged or have not been logged for hundreds or thousands of years; old-growth forests are mature ecosystems.

organ A group of tissues that forms a distinct structure and performs a specialized task, such as a heart in animals or a leaf in plants.

organic molecule Any molecule containing carbon. Such molecules usually are part of, or are derived from, living organisms.

overfishing The taking of so many fish from a fishery that the fish population cannot replenish itself.

overstory The uppermost foliage in a forest, rising above the canopy.

ozone A molecule composed of three oxygen atoms and symbolized as O_3. Ozone is a pollutant in the lower atmosphere, but in the upper atmosphere, it protects life on the Earth's surface from the Sun's deadly ultraviolet radiation.

ozone hole A "hole" in the ozone layer where ozone concentrations are diminished; the term usually refers to the Antarctic ozone hole.

parasite Organisms that obtain nourishment from a host organism; parasites may or may not harm their host, but they are not beneficial to it.

particulates Solid or liquid pollutants that are small enough to stay suspended in the air. They are generally nontoxic but can seriously reduce visibility.

pathogen Microorganisms—primarily bacteria, viruses, parasites, and toxic algae—that cause disease.

PCBs (polychlorinated biphenyls) Extremely stable, water-soluble, persistent organic pollutants that bioaccumulate and are found globally.

photosynthesis The process in which plants use carbon dioxide and water to produce sugar and oxygen. The simplified chemical reaction is $6CO_2 + 12H_2O + solar\ energy = C_6H_{12}O_6 + 6O_2 + 6H_2O$.

phytoplankton Microscopic, plantlike, usually single-celled organisms found at the surface of the ocean; they are the planet's single greatest source of oxygen.

plate tectonics The theory that the Earth's surface is divided into plates that move on the planet's surface and are driven by mantle convection.

Pleistocene The most recent ice age in Earth history (also referred to as the Ice Age), from between 2 million and 10,000 years before the present. The Pleistocene consisted of four glacial and three interglacial periods.

prairie Biome composed mostly of grasses, where summers are warm and winters are very cold; large herd animals roam the prairies of Australia, Africa, and North America.

predator An organism that kills and eats other animals for food energy.

primary producer An organism that produces food energy from inorganic substances; the term usually refers to a photosynthesizing plant but can also be used to describe chemosynthetic bacteria.

primary productivity The food energy created by producers.

prokaryote A single-celled organism with no membrane around its nucleus and very simple internal structure; organisms of the Kingdom Monera, such as bacteria and blue-green algae, are prokaryotes.

reproduction A feature of living things that allows them to give rise to new systems similar to themselves; reproduction may be asexual or sexual.

respiration The process by which an organism exchanges gases with the environment.

restoration ecology   The field of biology that seeks to restore an ecosystem that has been degraded, damaged, or destroyed; its goal is to reestablish biological community and ecosystem processes that were once native to an ecosystem and set up the land for sustainable use only.

runoff   Water that trickles across roadways and rooftops, and filters through landfills and soil; it often drains directly into streams or lakes.

scavenger   An animal that eats dead plants or animals for food energy.

scientific method   Research method used in science in which a problem is identified, data are gathered, a hypothesis is formulated, the hypothesis is tested, and, if it holds up, the hypothesis becomes a theory.

scientific name   A name used by scientists to identify an organism; it consists of genus and species names.

slash-and-burn agriculture   A method whereby rain forest plants in the tropics are slashed down and then burned to clear the land for agriculture.

speciation   The formation of a new species, usually resulting from some type of separation that keeps a population from breeding with its parent population.

species   A classification of organisms that includes those that can or do interbreed and produce fertile offspring; members of a species share the same gene pool.

sustainable   Word used to describe resource use that does not compromise the current needs for resources or the needs of future generations for present economic gain.

swamp   Poorly drained region where the water table lies above the ground surface.

symbiosis   A relationship in which organisms from different species habitually live together, usually to the benefit of both species.

temperate forest   Cool, wet biome with evergreen (including giant redwoods and Douglas fir) and deciduous (including maples and ash) forests and diverse mammals.

theory   An explanation for a natural phenomenon that is supported by virtually all data and that has no inconsistencies. It may be used to predict future events.

thermophilic   Heat-loving; thermophilic bacteria grow best at temperatures between 120°F (50°C) and 140°F (60°C).

threatened species   A species that is likely to become endangered in the future.

tissue   Within an organism, an aggregate of cells having a similar structure and function.

tributyltin (TBT)   A tin-containing compound that is an effective antifouling agent and an endocrine disruptor.

trophic level   Energy level within the food web; primary producers make up the first trophic level; the herbivores that eat the primary producers make up the second; the carnivores that eat the herbivores make up the third, and so on.

tundra   Biome of the polar regions and high altitudes, where low-lying, scrubby plants survive against the frigid cold, wind, and short growing season.

ultraviolet radiation (UV)   Shortwave, high energy solar radiation; the highest energy wavelengths of UV are extremely harmful to life.

understory   The shrub layer of a rain forest, between the canopy and the forest floor; because little light penetrates the canopy, the plant life of the understory is usually sparse.

vascular plant   Plants with roots, stems, leaves, vascular tissue for transporting water and food, and a cuticle that helps them resist desiccation (drying out).

vertebrate   An animal with a backbone; fish, amphibians, reptiles, birds, and mammals are all vertebrates.

vestigial structures   Nonfunctional or partly functional remnants of organs that are evolutionary leftovers, no longer useful for whatever function they served for the organisms' evolutionary ancestors; horses walk on the middle toe, with nonfunctional second and fourth toes up their hooves.

virus Tiny life forms composed mainly of nucleic acid with a protein coat. Viruses must use a host's cells to reproduce and so are, by definition, parasites.

water vapor Water (H_2O) in its gaseous state.

watershed A river and all of its tributaries and all of the land that they drain.

wetland A poorly drained region that is covered all or part of the time with fresh or salt water.

zooplankton Tiny marine animals that are unable to swim on their own and instead drift with the currents.

Further Reading

Allen, William. *Green Phoenix: Restoring the Tropical Forests of Guanacaste, Costa Rica*. New York: Oxford University Press, 2001.

Archibald, J. David. "No, It Only Finished Them Off." *Natural History* 114 (May 2005): 52–54.

Blaustein, Andrew R., and Andy Dobson. "Extinctions: A Message from the Frogs." *Nature* 439 (January 2006): 439.

Boulter, Michael. *Extinction: Evolution and the End of Man*. New York: Columbia University Press, 2002.

Burdick, Alan. "How Does a Deer Cross the Road? (The Ecology of . . . Roadkill)." *Discover* (March 2004). Available online. URL: http://www.aburdick.com/articles.html.

_____. *Out of Eden: An Odyssey of Ecological Invasion*. New York: Farrar, Straus, and Giroux, 2005.

Derr, Mark. "Lure of the Exotic Stirs Trouble in the Animal Kingdom." *The New York Times*, February 12, 2002.

Elegant, Simon. "Eating Disorder: China's Appetite for Exotic Wildlife Has Spawned a Thriving Black Market in Asia's Endangered Species. Will Pangolin Be Eaten into Extinction?" *Time International (Asia Edition)* 166 (October 2005): 40.

Furniss, Charlie. "Taking Bushmeat off the Menu." *Geographical* 77 (January 2005): 69–73.

Ginsburg, Janet. "Where the Wild Things Are (Here)." *The Scientist* 18 (September 13, 2004): 12.

_____. "Dinner, Pets, and Plagues by the Bucketful: The Burgeoning Trade in Wild Animals Is Leading to an Ecodisaster." *The Scientist* 18 (April 12, 2004): 28–29

Hallam, Tony. *Catastrophes and Lesser Calamities: The Causes of Mass Extinctions.* Oxford: Oxford University Press, 2004.

Hamashige, Hope. "Drought Causing Record Forest Destruction in U.S. Southwest." *National Geographic News* (December 5, 2005). Available online. URL: http://news.nationalgeographic.com/news/2005/12/1205 _051205_drought_forest.html.

Hull, Jeff. "The Final Frontier." *Audubon* 107 (September–October 2005): 49–49.

Janzen, Daniel. "Costa Rica's Area de Conservación Guanacaste: A Long March to Survival Through Non-Damaging Biodevelopment." *Biodiversity* 1(2):7–20.

_____. "Gardenification of Wildland Nature and the Human Footprint." *Science*: 279(5355) (February 1998): 1312–1313.

_____. "Hotspots: Earths Biologically Richest and Most Endangered Terrestrial Ecoregions (Review)." *Quarterly Review of Biology* 75 (September 2001): 327.

Kareiva, Peter, and Michelle Marvier. "Conserving Biodiversity Coldspots: Recent Calls to Direct Conservation to the World's Biodiversity Hotspots May Be Bad Investment Advice." *American Scientist* 91 (July–August 2003): 344–351.

Kirby, Alex. "Biodiversity: The Sixth Wave." British Broadcasting Service (BBC). Available online. URL: http://news.bbc.co.uk/1/hi/sci/tech/ 3667300.stm. Accessed April 2, 2007.

Lovgren, Stefan. "Chimps, Humans 96 Percent the Same, Gene Study Finds." *National Geographic News* (August 2005). Available online. URL: http://news.nationalgeographic.com/news/2005/08/0831_050831 _chimp_genes.html. Accessed April 2, 2007.

Milius, Susan. "Bushmeat on the Menu: Untangling the Influences of Hunger, Wealth, and International Commerce." *Science News* 167 (February 26 2005): 138–142.

Morell, Virginia. "The Sixth Extinction." *National Geographic* (February 1999). Available online. URL: http://www.nationalgeographic.com/ ngm/9902/fngm/. Accessed April 2, 2007.

Myers, Norman. "Biodiversity Hotspots Revisited." *BioScience* 53 (October 2003): 916–918.

Nevala, Amy E. "Little Squirts Big Trouble: Invasive Species Smothers Everything in Its Path and Poses Threat to Fisheries." *Oceanus* 44 (June 2005): 28–29. Available online. URL: http://www.whoi.edu/oceanus/viewArticle.do?id=3940. Accessed April 2, 2007.

Nielsen, John. *Condor: To the Brink and Back—The Life and Times of One Giant Bird.* New York: HarperCollins, 2006.

Parmesan, Camille and Gary Yohe. "A Globally Coherent Fingerprint of Climate Change Impacts Across Natural Systems." *Nature* 421 (2003): 37–42.

Pound, J. Alan, and Robert Puschendorf. "Ecology: Clouded Futures." *Nature* 427 (2004): 107–109.

Public Broadcasting Service (PBS). "Evolution: A Journey into Where We're From and Where We're Going." WGBH/NOVA Science Unit and Clear Blue Sky Productions. Available online. URL: http://www.pbs.org/wgbh/evolution/index.html. Accessed April 2, 2007.

Robinson Robert A., et al. "Climate Change and Migratory Species." *BTO Research Report* 414 (August 2005). British Trust for Ornithology. Available online. URL: http://www.defra.gov.uk/wildlife-countryside/resprog/findings/climatechange-migratory/. Accessed April 2, 2007.

Rohter, Larry. "A Record Amazon Drought, and Fear of Wider Ills." *The New York Times*, December 11, 2005.

Shoumantoff, Alex. "Madame Butterfly." *Audubon* 107 (Sept–Oct 2005): 58–65.

Thomas, Chris D., et al. "Extinction Risk from Climate Change." *Nature* 427 (January 2004): 145–148.

Tyson, Neil deGrasse. "Knock 'Em Dead: How Does One Extinguish Life on Earth? Let Me Count the Ways." *Natural History* 114 (May 2005): 25–29.

United Nations Environment Programme (UNEP). "Living Beyond Our Means: Natural Assets and Human Well-being." Available online. http://www.millenniumassessment.org/en/Reports.aspx. Accessed April 2, 2007.

Wilson, E.O., Paul R. Ehrlich, Stuart Pimm, Peter H. Raven, et al. Letter to Honorable Senator Lincoln Chafee and Honorable Senator Hillary Rodham Clinton. Available online: http://www.saveesa.org/letter.pdf. Accessed April 2, 2007.

Zeller, Frank. "Buy Now, and Save! Preserving South American Wilderness—By Buying It Up." *World Watch* 18 (July–August 2005): 24–30.

Web Sites

Area de Conservación Guanacaste (ACG)
http://www.acguanacaste.ac.cr/1997/principaling.html
All about ACG, in English or Spanish.

Center for Biological Diversity
http://www.sw-center.org/swcbd/
*Protecting endangered species and wild places; affiliated with the
University of Arizona.*

Children's Eternal Rain Forest
http://www.acmcr.org/rain_forest.htm
*A Costa Rican rain forest that has been preserved by children and adults
throughout the world.*

Conservation International: Biodiversity Hotspots
http://www.biodiversityhotspots.org/xp/Hotspots
*A survey of biodiversity hotspots, which are locations with remarkable
biodiversity that are being threatened by habitat loss.*

**Convention on International Trade in Endangered Species of Wild Fauna
and Flora (CITES)**
http://www.cites.org/
About the convention, how it works, and which species are included.

U.S. Fish and Wildlife Service: The Endangered Species Program
http://www.fws.gov/endangered/
Information about the Endangered Species Program.

**International Union for Conservation of Nature and Natural Resources
(IUCN) Red List of Threatened Species**
http://www.redlist.org
The latest IUCN Red List of Threatened Species.

Marine Aquarium Council

http://www.aquariumcouncil.org

International certification for the quality and sustainability of marine organisms.

Mongabay.com

http://www.mongabay.com/home.htm

Rain forest information for adults and kids, with a special section on Madagascar.

Rincon Rainforest

http://janzen.sas.upenn.edu/caterpillars/RR/rincon_rainforest.htm

The effort to save the Rincon Rainforest.

TRAFFIC

http://www.traffic.org

The wildlife trade monitoring network Web site.

United Nations Environment Programme (UNEP): Global Environment Outlook

http://www.unep.org/GEO/geo3/english/219.htm

"GEO-3: Global Environment Outlook." Global and regional perspectives on biodiversity.

United Nations Educational, Scientific, and Cultural Organization (UNESCO): People, Biodiversity and Ecology

http://www.unesco.org/mab/index.shtml

The Man and the Biosphere (MAB) Programme and biosphere reserves.

World Conservation Union

http://www.iucn.org

From the World Conservation Union, information about biodiversity and the effects humans have on biodiversity.

Index

About the Author

DANA DESONIE, PH.D., has written about the earth, ocean, space, life, and environmental sciences for more than a decade. Her work has appeared in educational lessons, textbooks, and magazines, and on radio and the Web. Her 1996 book, *Cosmic Collisions*, described the importance of asteroids and comets in Earth history and the possible consequences of a future asteroid collision with the planet. Before becoming a science writer, she received a doctorate in oceanography, spending weeks at a time at sea, mostly in the tropics, and one amazing day at the bottom of the Pacific in the research submersible *Alvin*. She now resides in Phoenix, Arizona, with her neuroscientist husband, Miles Orchinik, and their two children.